The Peeragogy Handbook

The Peeragogy Handbook

Founding Editor
Howard Rheingold

Editorial Board
George Brett, Joseph Corneli, Charles Jeffrey Danoff,
Kyle Larson, Charlotte Pierce, Paola Ricaurte, Fabrizio Terzi

with contributions from
Bryan Alexander, Paul Allison, María Fernanda Arenas,
Régis Barondeau, Doug Breitbart, Suz Burroughs,
Teryl Cartwright, Jay Cross, Julian Elve,
James Folkestad, Kathy Gill, John Glass,
John Graves, Jan Herder, Gigi Johnson,
Anna Keune, Roland Legrand, Amanda Lyons,
Christopher Neal, Ted Newcomb, Stephanie Parker,
David Preston, Stephanie Schipper, Peter Taylor,
and Geoff Walker

Friday 21st March, 2014 (version 2.01)

All the text in this book has been donated to the
Public Domain.

SMALL CAPS correspond to links in the online version
of the book, which is at HTTP://PEERAGOGY.ORG.

ISBN: 978-0-9776396-4-9

Cover: Fabrizio Terzi & Charlotte Pierce
Illustrations: Amanda Lyons

Typeset in Linux Libertine with X_ƎLaTeX.
Sources available at HTTP://GIT.IO/HANDBOOK.

Jointly published by Pierce Press and PubDomEd.

Contents

Foreword 1

I Introduction 5
1 Welcome! 7
2 How to use this handbook 9
3 Chapter Summaries 13

II Peer Learning 19
4 An Overview 21

III Motivation 41
5 Why we're doing this 43
6 Case Study: 5PH1NX 49

IV Peeragogy in Practice 63
7 Thinking about patterns 65
8 Patterns 73
9 Antipatterns 83
10 A pattern story 91

V Convening A Group 93
11 Convening 95
12 Play and learning 103

13	K-12 Peeragogy	107
14	P2P SOLE	111
15	A story about new beginnings	121

VI Organizing a Learning Context   123

16	Organizing Co-Learning	125
17	Adding structure	135
18	The student authored syllabus	141
19	How to Organize a MOOC	151
20	Case Study: Collaborative Explorations	159

VII Cooperation   169

21	Co-facilitation	171
22	The Workscape	175
23	Participation	179
24	Designs for co-working	183
25	A co-working story	193

VIII Assessment   195

26	Peeragogical Assessment	197
27	Researching Peeragogy	207

IX Technologies, Services, and Platforms   215

28	Peeragogy Technology	217
29	Forums	229
30	Wiki	233
31	Real-time Meetings	241

X Resources   247

32 How to get involved   249
33 Peeragogy in Action   253
34 Recommended Reading   261
35 Style Guide   271
36 Meet the Authors   275
37 Web Pages Cited in This Book 285
38 License/Waiver   309

FOREWORD

I was invited to lecture at UC Berkeley in January, 2012, and to involve their faculty and their graduate students in some kind of seminar, so I told the story of how I've used social media in teaching and learning - and invited them to help me create a handbook for self-learners.

I called it the Peeragogy Handbook. I met twice on the Berkeley campus in the weeks following the lecture with about a dozen Berkeley faculty and graduate students. We also had a laptop open with Elluminate, an online platform that enabled video chatting and text chat, enabling people around the world who were interested in the subject, who I recruited through Twitter and email, to also participate in this conversation. All of the faculty and grad students at Berkeley dropped out of the project, but we ended up with about two dozen people, most of them educators, several of them students, in Canada, Belgium, Brazil, Germany, Italy, Mexico, the UK, USA, and Venezuela who ended up collaborating on a voluntary effort to create this Peeragogy Handbook, at peeragogy.org. We all shared an interest in the question: "If you give more and more of your power as a teacher to the students, can't you just eliminate the teacher all together, or can't people take turns being the facilitator of the class?"

Between the time nine years ago, when I started out using social media in teaching and learning, clearly there's been an explosion of people learning things together online via Wikipedia and YouTube, MOOCs and Quora, Twitter and Facebook, Google Docs and video chat, and I don't really know what's going to happen with the institutions, but I do know that this wild learning is happening and that some people are becoming more expert at it.

I started trying to learn programming this summer, and I think that learning programming and doing programming must be very, very different now from before the Web, because now, if you know the right question to ask, and you put it into a search query, there's someone out there on StackOverflow who is already discussing it. More and more people are getting savvy to the fact that you don't have to go to a university to have access to all of the materials, plus media that the universities haven't even had until recently. What's missing for learners outside formal institutions who know how to use social media is useful lore about how people learn together without a teacher. Nobody should ever overlook the fact that there are great teachers. Teachers should be trained, rewarded, and sought out. But it's time to expand the focus on learners, particularly on self-learners whose hunger for learning hasn't been schooled out of them.

I think that we're beginning to see the next step, which is to develop the methods – we certainly have the technologies, accessible at the cost of broadband access – for self-learners to teach and learn from each other more effectively. Self-learners know how to go to YouTube, they know how to use search, mobilize personal learning networks. How does a group of self-learners organize co-learning?

In the Peeragogy project, we started with a WIKI and then we decided that we needed to have a mechanism for people who were self-electing to write articles on the wiki to say, OK, this is ready for editing, and then for an editor to come in and say, this is ready for Wordpress, and then for someone to say, this has been moved to WordPress. We used a forum to hash out these issues and met often via Elluminate, which enabled us to all use audio and video, to share screens, to text-chat, and to simultaneously draw on a whiteboard. We tried Piratepad for a while. Eventually we settled on WordPress as our publication platform and moved our most of our discussions to Google+. It was a messy process, learning to work together while deciding what, exactly it was we were doing and how we were going to go about it. In the end we ended up evolving methods and settled on tools that worked pretty well. We tackled key questions and provided resources for dealing with them: How you want to govern your learning community? What kinds of technologies do you want to use, and why, and how to use them? How are learners going to convene, what kind of resources are available, and are those resources free or what are their advantages and disadvantages. We were betting that if we could organize good responses to all these questions, a resource would prove to be useful: Here's a resource on how to organize a syllabus or a learning space, and here are a lot of suggestions for good learning activities, and here's why I should use a wiki rather than a forum. We planned the Handbook to be an open and growable resource – if you want to add to it, join us! The purpose of all this work is to provide a means of lubricating the process of creating online courses and/or learning spaces.

Please use this handbook to enhance your own peer learning and please join our effort to expand and enhance its value. The people who came together to create the first edition – few of us knew any of the others, and often people from three continents would participate in our synchronous meetings – found that creating the Handbook was a training course and experiment in peeragogy. If you want to practice peeragogy, here's a vehicle. Not only can you use it, you can expand it, spread it around. Translators have already created versions of the first edition of the handbook in Spanish, and Italian, and work is in progress to bring these up to date with the second edition. We've recently added a Portuguese translation team: more translators are welcome.

What made this work? Polycentric leadership is one key. Many different members of the project stepped up at different times and in different ways and did truly vital things for the project. Currently, over 30 contributors have signed the CC Zero waiver and have material in the handbook; over 600 joined our Peeragogy in Action community on G+; and over 1000 tweets mention peeragogy.org. People clearly like the concept of peeragogy – and a healthy number also like participating in the process.

We know that this isn't the last word. We hope it's a start. We invite new generations of editors, educators, learners, media-makers, web-makers, and translators to build on our foundation.

Howard Rheingold
Marin County
January, 2014

Part I

Introduction

CHAPTER 1

WELCOME TO THE PEERAGOGY HANDBOOK

Welcome to the Peeragogy Handbook!
Peeragogy is a collection of techniques for collaborative learning and collaborative work. By learning how to "work smart" together, we hope to leave the world in a better state than it was when we arrived.

Indeed, humans have always learned from each other. But for a long time – until the advent of the Web and widespread access to digital media – schools have had an effective monopoly on the business of learning. Now, with access to open educational resources and free or inexpensive communication platforms, groups of people can learn together outside as well as inside formal institutions. All of this prompted us to reconsider the meaning of "peer learning."

The *Peeragogy Handbook* isn't a normal book. It is an evolving guide, and it tells a collaboratively written story that *you* can help write. Using this book, you will develop new norms for the groups you work with — whether online, offline, or both. Every section includes practical ideas you can apply to build and sustain strong and exciting collaborations. When you read the book, you will get to know the authors and will see how we have applied these ideas: in classrooms, in research, in business, and more.

You'll meet Julian, one of the directors of a housing association; Roland, a professional journalist and change-maker; Charlie, a language teacher and writer who works with experimental media for fun and profit; and Charlotte, an indie publisher who wants to become better at what she does by helping others learn how to do it well too — as well as many other contributors from around the globe.

The book focuses on techniques for convening a strong group, organizing a learning space, doing cooperative work, and conducting effective peer assessment. These major sections are complemented by a catalog of design patterns and notes on relevant technologies.

The next section is a guide to using the book, but, in brief, if you're reading this book on peeragogy.org, please use the comment feature to share your thoughts, and if you're reading it on paper, get out your pen and start making notes. The best way to get something out of Peeragogy is to put a lot into it. We are always interested in more case studies, and anything that will improve the presentation and usefulness of this material, so please don't hesitate to get in touch.

CHAPTER 2

HOW TO USE THIS HANDBOOK

This document is a practical guide to co-learning, a living document that invites comment and invites readers to join the community of editors. The document does not have to be read in linear order from beginning to end. Material about conceptualizing and convening co-learning – the stuff that helps with getting started – is located toward the top of the table of contents. Material about use cases, resources, and assessment is located toward the bottom. Hop around if you'd like.

We've focused on "hands-on" techniques, and you'll probably want to try things out with your own groups and networks as you read.

- If you want a starter syllabus, check out "Peeragogy in Action" in the resources section.

- If you want to delve directly into the research literature, our initial literature survey forms the basis of a WIKIPEDIA ARTICLE, and the book also includes additional recommended readings.

- For something lighter, many pages in the online version of the book include short introductory videos, most of them under one minute long. You can do a SEARCH ON YOUTUBE to find these and many of our other videos all in one place.

This is a living document. If you want to join in, just let us know in our G+ COMMUNITY. (which also happens to have the name *Peeragogy in Action*). If you want to test the waters first, feel free to use the comment thread attached to each page on peeragogy.org to suggest any changes or additions, and to share a bit about your story. We might quote you in future versions of the book to help improve the resource for others, like this:

John Glass: Reading through the handbook, it strikes me that the users will be fairly sophisticated folks. They will have ample knowledge of various tech platforms, resources, a fair amount of formal education, access and ability to use a number of different gadgets. My dilemma is that I am thinking that Peeragogy, at its most basic, seems to be about facilitating P2P learning. As such, at its most basic, it would be about assisting people to work together to learn something (and for me, learning encompasses virtually all human behavior, with the possible exception of that controlled by the autonomic nervous system and even there I am not sure). In other words, I am thinking it is about helping anyone learn through partnership with others (group *A*) and yet the handbook appears to be geared toward a rather specialized group of people (group *B*). I guess what I am looking for is perhaps some clarification on who is the intended audience, *A* or *B*? As it stands, I am unsure how it could realistically apply to *A*...Thanks.

Joe Corneli: I think that the best thing to do is to do this in dialog. In addition to groups *A* and *B*, we might need a group *C*, who would mediate between the two. The assignment would be something like this: "Use this to structure the class, and if you get stuck at any point or if you think the resource isn't the right one, ask me for help, and we'll work on finding other solutions together." At the end of the semester, you might have a new and very different book tailored to this particular "audience" (or "public" to use Howard's term)! That would be cool. The current book definitely isn't a one-size-fits-all – I'd say it's more like a sewing machine. In fact, I think group *C* is the real "public" for this book – not experts, but people who will say: "How can I use the ideas and the process here to do something new?" What people do with it will definitely depend on the goal: the model might be *Stand and Deliver* or it might be *Good Will Hunting* or it may be something very different. Our long-term goal is not to build a 1000 page version of the handbook, but to serve as a "hub" that can help many different peer learning projects. The first question is: How can we improve the usability for you? Rather than tackling the whole book all at once, I would recommend that we start by dialoging about the "Peeragogy in Action" syllabus at the end. How would we have to tailor that to suit the needs of your students? With that in mind, another useful starting point might be our article on the student authored syllabus. Finally, our motto for the book is: "*This is a How-To Handbook.*" We can talk more about anything that's confusing and get rid of or massively revise anything that's not useful. That's a super-micro guide to doing peeragogy.

CHAPTER 3

CHAPTER SUMMARIES

Peering into Learning

This is a quick introduction to the main ideas used in the rest of the book. It provides a range of things to think about as you get started with a new peer learning project, or as you use peeragogy to redesign and reassess an existing collaboration. You'll probably want to read this first and then do some reflection before diving into the other parts of the book.

Motivation

You might wonder why we're doing this project – what we hope to get out of it as volunteers, and how we think what we're doing can make a positive difference in the world. Have a look at this chapter if you, too, are thinking about getting involved in peeragogy, or wondering how peeragogy can help you accelerate your own learning projects.

Case Study: 5PH1NX. We enjoy riddles with more than one answer, so we've included this detailed narrative example of peeragogy in action near the beginning of the book. We hope you are inspired by the challenge of doing peeragogy in a school setting that is recounted here. Explore this case study for ideas and encouragement for your own learning adventures.

Patterns, use cases, examples

Here we show you some of the signposts that can serve as both a key and compass to the kind of social problem solving that happens in peeragogy projects. If you want some underlying components to try out, mix and match these and experiment with peeragogy right away. You come back to this chapter for a deeper understanding of the processes we talk about later on. A detailed catalog of patterns and anti-patterns that we've drawn from our own practice form a core part of the book.

Convening a Group

You'll probably want to use this chapter to organize your thinking as you start a new peeragogy project or think about how to apply peeragogy ideas in an existing collaboration. A few clusters of simple but important questions will inspire unique answers for you and your group. We hope these mental frameworks are helpful to not only initiate progress, but also to maintain momentum.

Play & Learning. What makes learning fun? Just as actors learn their roles through the dynamic process of performance, In other words, the more we engage with a topic, the better we learn it and the more satisfying - or fun - the process becomes.

K-12 Peeragogy. The key to becoming a successful 'connected educator-learner' involves spending the time needed to learn how to learn and share in an open, connected environment. Once you make the decision to enter into a dialogue with another user, you become a connected educator/learner and tap into the power of networks to distribute the load of learning. Depending on their age, you can even facilitate an awareness of peer networks among your students.

P2P Self-Organizing Learning Environments. This conversational section engages you in a journey through diverse points of entry that interact with your physical learning space. Within this chapter of word and picture images, the emerging structure and reciprocal mentoring that may be inspired causes a ripple effect on those who open the door to its possibilities.

Organizing a Learning Context

We talk about how peer learning is organized into "courses" and "spaces", again drawing on our experience in the peeragogy project. We present the results of an informal poll that reveals some of the positive and some of the negative features of our early choices.

Adding Structure with Activities. The first rule of thumb for peer learning is: announce activities only when you plan to take part as a fully engaged participant. Then ask a series of questions: what is the goal, what makes it challenging, what worked in other situations, what recipe is appropriate, what is different about learning about this topic?

Student Authored Syllabus. Here's one place you might explore to see ways in which freedom in student-directed learning complements the structural needs for the content and group. Check this out for various methods to welcome ambiguity and co-created curriculum into your projects. You may want to start with one or two ideas in an activity to transition into this format, yet embracing the risk on a larger scale is fun as well.

Connectivism in Practice. Massive Open Online Courses (MOOCs) are decentralized online learning experiences: individuals and groups create blogs or wikis and comment on each other's work, often with a focus on where to find information. A course typically has a topic, activities, reading resources and a guest speaker for each week. Items are tagged to allow for aggregation. Links to technology resources are provided (such as gRSShopper from Stephen Downes).

Case Study: Collaborative Explorations. You can try out this chapter to encourage individuals pursuing their own interests in a predetermined topic while at the same time influencing the learning of the whole group by sharing and reflecting upon their findings. These interactions of supportive mutual inquiry evolve the content and structure within a short time frame and with open-ended results.

Cooperation

Sometimes omitting the figurehead empowers a group. Co-facilitation tends to work in groups of people who gather to share common problems and experiences. The chapter suggests how to co-facilitate discussions, wiki workflows, and live sessions. Conducting an "after action review" helps to avoid blind spots.

The Workscape. In a corporate workscape, people are free-range learners: protect the learning environment, provide nutrients for growth, and let nature take its course. A workscape features profiles, an activity stream, wikis, virtual meetings, blogs, bookmarks, mobile access and a social network.

Participation. Participation grows from having a community of people who learn together, using a curriculum as a starting point to organize and trigger engagement. Keep in mind that participation may follow the 90/9/1 principle (lurkers/editors/authors) and that people may transition through these roles over time.

New Designs For Co-Working And Co-Learning. Designing for peer learning requires a new approach. A case study dealing focusing on PlanetMath shows one way to go.

Assessment

Asking questions about assessment in the context of the Handbook (Who needs to know? Based on what data? In what format?) suggests "usefulness" (real problems solved) is an appropriate metric. We use the idea of return on investment (the value of changes in behavior divided by the cost of inducing the change) to assess the peeragogy project itself, as one example.

Researching peeragogy. Three new patterns are introduced (Frontend and Backend, Spanning Set, and Minimum Viable Project) which form the basis of a "meta-model" that can be used to study and design for peer learning.

Technologies, Services, and Platforms

Issues of utility, choice, coaching, impact and roles attach to the wide variety of tools and technologies available for peer learning. Keys to selection include the features you need, what people are already using, and the type of tool (low threshold, wide wall, high ceilings) used for collaboration.

Forums. Forums are web-based communication media that enable groups of people to conduct organized multimedia discussions about multiple topics over a period of time, asynchronously. A rubric for evaluating forum posts highlights the value of drawing connections. The chapter includes tips on selecting forum software.

Wiki. A wiki is a website whose users can add, modify, or delete its content via a web browser. Pages have a feature called "history" which allows users to see previous versions and roll back to them. The chapter includes tips on how to use a wiki and select a wiki engine, with particular attention to peer learning opportunities.

Real-time meetings. Web services enable broadband-connected learners to communicate in real time via audio, video, slides, whiteboards, chat, and screen-sharing. Possible roles for participants in real-time meetings include searchers, contextualizers, summarizers, lexicographers, mappers, and curators. This mode of interaction supports emergent agendas.

Resources

Here we present several ways to get involved in peer learning, including information about where to find the Peeragogy project online, a sample syllabus with four actions bring peer learning to life, tips on writing for The Handbook, and our Creative Commons Zero 1.0 Universal (CC0 1.0) Public Domain Dedication.

Part II

Peer Learning

CHAPTER 4

AN OVERVIEW OF PEER LEARNING

The aim of the *Peeragogy Handbook* is to establish effective peer-learning techniques that you can implement "on the ground." We suggest that you look through the Handbook, try a few of these suggestions, and see how they work for you. Then we invite you share your experiences, ask for feedback, and work with us to improve the Handbook and the field we affectionately call "Peeragogy."

In this part of the *Peeragogy Handbook*, we "peeragogues" have summarised the most important and applicable research and insights from two years of inquiry and discussion. Although there's been no shortage of experimentation and formal research into collaborative, connective, and shared learning systems in the past, there is a new rumbling among education thinkers that suggests that when combined with new platforms and technologies, peer-learning strategies as described here could have a huge impact on the way educational institutions evolve in the future. We've also seen for ourselves how peer-learning techniques can help anyone who's interested to become a more effective informal educator.

The interplay of individual and group

"Personal" supports "peer". We can consciously cultivate living, growing, responsive webs of information, support, and inspiration that help us be more effective learners. This is known as a personal learning network. We'll offer tips on how to build these networks — and we'll also explain how strong personal learning networks can contribute to and evolve into even stronger peer learning networks.

"Peer" supports "personal". As we work together to develop shared plans for our collective efforts in group projects, we usually can find places where we have something to learn. Furthermore, if we are willing to ask for help and offer our help to others, everybody's learning escalates. Being mindful of effective interpersonal learning patterns is an important part of building an effective personal learning plan.

Peer learning through the ages

As you will have guessed, our new term, peeragogy, is a riff on the word pedagogy — the art, science, or profession of teaching. Pedagogy has a somewhat problematic origin: it comes from the ancient Greek tradition of having a child (paidos) be supervised (agogos) by a slave. Greek philosophers seem to have disagreed about to the best way for individuals to gain knowledge (and even more so, wisdom). Socrates, who insisted that he was not wise, also insisted that his interlocutors join him in investigating truth claims, as peers. And yet, Plato, the most famous of these interlocutors and the best-known author of Socratic dialogs, in his most famous allegory of the cave, has Socrates say, with a modest but clearly pedagogical bent:

> **Socrates**: This entire allegory, I said, you may now append, dear Glaucon, to the previous argument; the prison-house is the world of sight, the light of the fire is the sun, and you will not misapprehend me if you interpret the journey upwards to be the ascent of the soul into the intellectual world according to my poor belief, which, at your desire, I have expressed—whether rightly or wrongly God knows. But, whether true or false, my opinion is that in the world of knowledge the idea of good appears last of all, and is seen only with an effort; and, when seen, is also inferred to be the universal author of all things

beautiful and right, parent of light and of the lord of light in this visible world, and the immediate source of reason and truth in the intellectual; and that this is the power upon which he who would act rationally either in public or private life must have his eye fixed.

In more recent centuries, various education theorists and reformers have challenged the effectiveness of what had become the traditional teacher-led model. Most famous of the early education reformers in the United States was John Dewey, who advocated new experiential learning techniques. In his 1916 book, *Democracy and Education* [1], Dewey wrote, "Education is not an affair of 'telling' and being told, but an active and constructive process." Soviet psychologist Lev Vygotsky, who developed the concept of the Zone of Proximal Development, was another proponent of "constructivist" learning. His book, *Thought and Language* [2] also gives evidence to support collaborative, socially meaningful, problem-solving activities as opposed to isolated exercises.

Within the last few decades, things have begun to change very rapidly. In "Connectivism: A Learning Theory for the Digital Age," George Siemens argues that technology has changed the way we learn, explaining how it tends to complicate or expose the limitations of the learning theories of the past [3]. The crucial point of connectivism is that the connections that make it possible for us to learn in the future are more relevant than the knowledge we hold individually in the present. Technology can, to some degree and in certain contexts, replace "know how" with "know where to look."

If you want more details on the history, theories, and recent experiments related to peer learning, we have a more extensive literature review available. We've also adapted it into a Wikipedia page, which you can edit as well as read.

From peer learning to peeragogy

The idea that we needed a new theory (which we initially gave the name "paragogy" [4]) arose out of the challenges we faced

PLATON CAVE SANRAEDAM (1604). By Jan Saenredam [Public domain], via Wikimedia Commons

doing peer learning. Our aim was to understand how groups and organizations can become better at serving participants' interests, while participants also learn and become better contributors.

Paragogy began as a set of proposed principles that describe peer produced peer learning – we'll say what these principles are just below. We designed them to contrast with a set guidelines for adult educators advanced by Malcolm Knowles [5]. The paragogy principles focus on the way in which co-learners shape their learning context together. Very likely, there will be no educator anywhere in sight. And just for this reason, peer produced peer learning is something for "innovative educators" everywhere. You don't need to have the word teacher, trainer, or educator in your job title. It's enough to ask good questions.

The paragogy principles aim to make that more explicit. They advocate for an approach to peer learning in which:

1. Changing context is a decentered center.

2. Meta-learning is a font of knowledge.

An Overview

3. Peers provide feedback that wouldn't be there otherwise.

4. Learning is distributed and nonlinear.

5. You realize the dream if you can, then wake up!

If some of these principles seem a bit ephemeral, it may help to think of in a more unified manner, as a set of dimensions that describe possible changes that can take place in peer produced peer learning [6]:

1. Changing the nature of the space

2. Changing what I know about myself

3. Changing my perspective

4. Changing content or connectivity

5. Changing objectives

Now that we've connecting the idea of paragogy to a perspective focused on the kinds of change that can take place in peer produced peer learning, it's time to reveal that our secret for success is hidden in plain view: the word "paragogy" means "production" in Greek. We're particularly interested in how the powerful blend of peer learning and collaborative work drives open source software development, and helps to build resources like Wikipedia. But in fact it works equally well in offline settings, from official hacker/maker spaces to garages and treehouses. Projects like STORYCORPS show how contemporary media can add a powerful new layer to ancient strategies for teaching, learning, and sharing.

The word "peeragogy" attempts to make these ideas immediately understandable to everyone, including non-geeks. Peeragogy is about peers learning together, and teaching each other. In the end, the two words are actually synonyms. If you want to go into theory-building mode, you can spell it "paragogy". If you want to be a bit more down to earth, stick with "peeragogy."

References

1. Dewey, J. (2004). Democracy and education. Dover Publications.

2. Vygotsky, L. S. (1986). Thought and language. MIT press.

3. Siemens, G. (2005). Connectivism: A learning theory for the digital age. International Journal of Instructional Technology and Distance Learning, 2(1), 3-10.

4. Corneli, J. and Danoff, C. J. (2011), Paragogy: Synergizing individual and organizational learning. (Published on Wikiversity.)

5. Knowles, M. S. (1980). The modern practice of adult education: From pedagogy to andragogy. Chicago: Follett.

6. Corneli, J. and Mikroyannidis, A. (2011). Personalised Peer-Supported Learning: The Peer-to-Peer Learning Environment (P2PLE). *Digital Education Review* 20, 14-23.

Which is more fun, skateboarding or physics?

Consider the following learning scenarios:

1. A small study group convenes at at the library late one night, resolving to do well on the next day's physics exam. The students manage to deflect their purpose for a while by gossiping about hook-ups and parties, studying for other classes, and sharing photos. Then, first one member, then another, takes the initiative and as a group, the students eventually pull their attention back to the task at hand. They endure the monotony of studying for several hours, and the next day, they own the exam.

2. A young skateboarder spends hours tweaking the mechanics of how to make a skateboard float in the air for a split second, enduring physical pain of repeated wipeouts. With repetition and success comes a deep understanding of the physics of the trick. That same student cannot string together more than five minutes of continuous attention during class and spends even less time on homework for the class before giving up.

Peer-learning participants succeed when they are motivated to learn. Skateboarding is primarily intrinsically motivated, with some extrinsic motivation coming from the respect that kids receive from peers when they master a trick. In most cases, the primary motivation for learning physics is extrinsic, coming from parents' and society's expectations that the student excel and assure his or her future by getting into a top college.

The student very well could be intrinsically motivated to have a glowing report card, but not for the joy of learning physics or chemistry, but because of the motivation to earn a high grade as part of her overall portfolio. Taken a different way, what is it about these topics that's fun for a student who loves science? Perhaps she anticipates the respect, power and prestige that comes from announcing a new breakthrough; or she may feel her work is important for the greater good, or prosperity, of humanity; or she may simply be thrilled to think about atoms bonding to form new compounds.

Learning situations frequently bore the learner when extrinsic motivation is involved. Whether by parents or society, being forced to do something, as opposed to choosing to, ends up making the individual less likely to succeed. In some cases it's clear, but trying to figure out what makes learning fun for a group of individual humans can be very difficult. Often there is no clear-cut answer that can be directly applied in the learning environment. Either way, identifying the factors that can make learning boring or fun is a good start. Perhaps learning certain skills or topics is intrinsically boring, no matter what, and we have to accept that.

Photo of Dmitri Mendeleev (1834-1907). Found on The Guardian's Notes & Theories blog. Public domain.

Learning patterns

One way to think about fun learning is that it's fun to learn - and be aware that you're learning - new patterns. Jürgen Schmidhuber wrote: "A [...] learner maximizes expected fun by finding or creating data that is better compressible in some yet unknown but learnable way, such as jokes, songs, paintings, or scientific observations obeying novel, unpublished laws" [1]. So the skateboarder enjoyed coming across new patterns: novel tricks that are learnable. (By the way, a few people, like mathematician William Stein, find ways to combine the love of science and skateboarding.)

Learner, know thyself: a self-evaluation technique

The learning contributed and acquired by each member of the peer learning enterprise depends on a healthy sense of self-awareness. When you ask yourself, "What do I have to offer?" and "What do I get out of it?" we think you'll come up with some exciting answers. In peer learning, whether or not you're pursuing a practical objective, you're in charge, and this kind of learning is usually fun. Indeed, as we'll describe below, there are deep links between play and learning. We believe we can improve the co-learning experience by adopting a playful mindset. Certainly some of our best learning moments in the Peeragogy project have been peppered with humor and banter. So we found that a key strategy for successful peer learning is to engage in a self-assessment of your motivations and abilities. In this exercise, you take into account factors like the learning context, timing and sequence of learning activities, social reinforcements, and visible reward. The peeragogical view is that learning is most effective when it contains some form of enjoyment or satisfaction, or when it leads to a concrete accomplishment.

When joining the Peeragogy project, Charles Jeffrey Danoff did a brief self-evaluation about what makes him interested in learning:

1. **Context**. I resist being groomed for some unforeseeable future rather than for a specific purpose.

2. **Timing and sequence**. I find learning fun when I'm studying something as a way to procrastinate on another pressing assignment.

3. **Social reinforcement**. Getting tips from peers on how to navigate a snowboard around moguls was more fun for me than my Dad showing me the proper way to buff the car's leather seats on chore day.

4. **Experiential awareness**. In high school, it was not fun to sit and compose a 30-page reading journal for Frankenstein. But owing in part to those types of prior experiences, I now find writing pleasurable and it's fun to learn how to write better.

We will explore the patterns of peer learning in more detail in the section on practice.

Reference

1. Schmidhuber, J. (2010). Formal theory of creativity, fun, and intrinsic motivation. Autonomous Mental Development (IEEE), 2(3), 230-247.

What kind of help do you need?

Personal Learning Networks are the collections of people and information resources (and relationships with them) that people cultivate in order to form their own public or private learning networks — living, growing, responsive sources of information, support, and inspiration that support self-learners.

> **Howard Rheingold**: "When I started using social media in the classroom, I looked for and began to learn from more experienced educators. First, I read and then tried to comment usefully on their blog posts and tweets. When I began to understand who knew what in the world of social media in education, I narrowed my focus to the most knowledgeable and adventurous among them. I paid attention to the people the savviest social media educators paid attention to. I added and subtracted voices from my attention network, listened and followed, then commented and opened conversations. When I found something I thought would interest the friends and strangers I was learning from, I passed along my own learning through my blogs and Twitter stream. I asked questions, asked for help, and eventually started providing answers and assistance to those who seemed to know less than I. The teachers I had been learning from had a name for what I was doing — "growing a personal learning network." So I started looking for and learning from people who talked about HOW to grow a "PLN" as the enthusiasts called them."

An Overview

Strong and weak ties

Your PLN will have people and sites that you check on often – your main sources of information and learning – your 'strong ties'. Your 'weak ties' are those people and sites that you don't allow a lot of bandwidth or time. But they may become strong later, as your network grows or your interests expand. This is a two-way street – it is very important that you are sharing what you learn and discover with those in your network and not just taking, if you want to see your network expand.

Explore	**How to Cultivate a Personal Learning Network**	Respond
Search		Inquire
Follow	Tips from Howard Rheingold	Engage
Tune		Feed

Peer learning networks

As you convene your peer learning group, in one form or another you will develop and share "peeragogical profiles" — advertising what you want to learn, what you'd be interested in helping teach others. If you present yourself and your projects in a thoughtful and engaging way, this will help you to build effective connections.

Networks of these connections can span across different subjects, across a city, or across national boundaries. Peeragogy helps to make sense of the idea of "learning networks" that has been around since at least the 1970s. Much as theories of pedagogy would be relevant for anyone carefully planning an individual learning programme, peeragogy is relevant for self-organized learning communities operating at larger scales.

How should we structure things?

From syllabus and curriculum to personal and peer learning plans

Part of the reason for the effectiveness of peeragogy is that the "syllabus" or "curriculum" – more generally, the learning plan – is developed by the people doing the learning. You won't faint with shock when you see the reading list if you helped write it.

Having youwn own learning plan at the outset helps each participant identify his or her unique learning and teaching proclivities and capabilities, and effectively apply them in the peer setting. In developing your personal plan, you can ask yourself the following questions:

1. What do I most need to learn about in the time ahead?

2. What are the best ways I learn, what learning activities will meet my learning needs, what help will I need and how long will it take?

3. What will I put into my personal portfolio to demonstrate my learning progress and achievements?

Early in the process, the peer learning group should also convene to develop a peer learning plan. In the Peeragogy project, we used live meetings and forum-style platforms to discuss the group-level versions of the questions listed above. Personal learning needs and skills were also aired via these platforms, but the key shared outcome was an initial project plan. Initially this took the form of an outline of handbook chapters to write, as well as a division of labor.

Nothing was set in stone, and both the peer group and individual participants have continued to develop, implement, review, and adjust their goals as the project develops. We have stayed sufficiently connected to the original goal of producing a handbook about peer learning that you now have one in your hands (or on your screen). We've also added some new goals for the project as time has gone by. Having a malleable framework enables peer learners to:

1. Identify appropriate directions and goals for future learning;

2. Review their strengths and areas for development;

3. Identify goals and plans for improvement;

4. Monitor their actions and review and adjust plans as needed to achieve their goals;

5. Update the goals to correspond to progress.

This doesn't mean you have to let chaos rule, but often in the swirl of ideas and contributions, new directions take shape and new ideas take hold.

Self-generating templates

Documentation like mind maps, outlines, blogs or journals, and forum posts for a peer learning project can create an audit trail or living history of the process. You can mine the documentation of a past peer-learning project or a completed phase of an ongoing project for effective learning patterns, and if you're careful to document everything, you can really benefit by taking the time to compare what you've achieved against the stated goal or mission at the outset. Use the record to reflect and evaluate key elements of the process for you as a facilitator and as a member of the peer learning group. Adapt your next phase of planning accordingly.

From corporate training to learning on the job

Today's knowledge workers typically have instant, ubiquitous access to the internet. The measure of their ability is an open-book exam. "What do you know?" is replaced with "What can you do?" And if they get bored, they can relatively easily be mentally elsewhere.

This has ramifications for the way managers manage as well as the way teachers teach. To extract optimal performance from workers, managers must inspire them rather than command them. Antoine de Saint-Exupéry put it nicely: "If you want to build a boat, do not instruct the men to saw wood, stitch the sails, prepare the tools and organize the work, but make them long for setting sail and travel to distant lands."

> **Jay Cross**: "If I were an instructional designer in a moribund training department, I'd polish up my resume and head over to marketing. Co-learning can differentiate services, increase product usage, strengthen customer relationships, and reduce the cost of hand-holding. It's cheaper and more useful than advertising. But instead of just making a copy of today's boring educational practices, build something based on interaction and camaraderie, perhaps with some healthy competition thrown in. Again, the emphasis should always be on learning in order to do something!"

In the section on organizing a learning context, we'll say quite a bit more about the implications that our full conception of peer learning has for managers, teachers, and other facilitators.

Can we work together on this?

Metacognition and mindfulness in peer learning

Metacognition and mindfulness have to do with your awareness how how you think, talk, participate, and attend to circumstances. It can be particularly useful to apply this sort of "meta awareness" as you think about the roles that you take on in a given project, the kind of contributions you want to make, and what you hope to get out of the experience. These are all likely to change as time passes, so it's good to get in the habit of reflection.

Potential roles in your peer-learning project

1. Leader, Manager, Team Member, Worker

2. Content Creator, Author, Content Processor, Reviewer, Editor

3. Presentation Creator, Designer, Graphics, Applications

4. Planner, Project Manager, Coordinator, Attendee, Participant

5. Mediator, Moderator, Facilitator, Proponent, Advocate, Representative, Contributor

Potential contributions

1. Create, Originate, Research, Aggregate

2. Develop, Design, Integrate, Refine, Convert

3. Write, Edit, Format

Potential motivations

1. Acquisition of training or support in a topic or field;

2. Building relationships with interesting people;

3. Finding professional opportunities through other participants;

4. Creating or bolstering a personal network;

A famous work in ink by Sengai Gibon (1750–1837)

5. More organized and rational thinking through dialog and debate;

6. Feedback about performance and understanding of the topic.

The process of shared reflection can prime a group for cohesion and success. It can be tremendously useful to think about the motivations of other participants, and how these can be jointly served. How can we re-use the "side-effects" of individual and cooperative efforts in a useful way?

Two theories of motivation

One of the most prominent thinkers working in the field of (self-)motivation is Daniel Pink [1], who proposes a theory of motivation based on autonomy, mastery, and purpose, or, more colorfully:

1. The urge to direct my life

2. The desire to get better at something that matters

An Overview

3. The yearning to do something that serves a purpose bigger than just "myself"

There's clearly a "learning orientation" behind the second point: it's not just a matter of "fun" — the sense of achievement matters. But fun remains relevant. Thomas Malone [2] specifically asked "What makes things fun to learn?" His proposed framework for building fun learning activities is also based on the three ingredients: fantasy, challenge, and curiosity.

We can easily see how "participation" relates to "motivation" as described above. When I can get useful information from other people, I can direct my own life better. When I have means of exploring my dreams by chatting then over and exploring some of the elements in a safe way, I'm in a much better position to make something in reality. A solid reputation that comes from being able to help others serves as a good indicator of personal progress, a sign that one is able to deal with greater challenges. Relationships provide the most basic sense of being part of something bigger than oneself: et cetera. We'll say more about these matters in the chapters on Cooperation.

References

1. Pink, D. (2011), Drive: The Surprising Truth About What Motivates Us, Canongate Books Ltd

2. Malone, T.W. (1981), Toward a Theory of Intrinsically Motivating Instruction, Cognitive Science, 4, pp. 333-369

How do we know if we've won?

Different ways to analyze the learning process

After doing some personal reflection on the roles you want to take on and the contributions you want to make (as we discussed above), you may also want to work together with your learning group to analyze the learning process in more detail. There are many different phases, stages, and dimensions - some simple and intuitive, others more complex – that you can use to help structure and understand the learning experience: we list some of these below. (Detailed references are collected in the recommended readings at the end of the book.)

1. Forming, Norming, Storming, Performing (from Bruce Tuckman)

2. The "five-stage e-moderating model" (from Gilly Salmon)

3. I, We, Its, It (from Ken Wilber – for an application in modeling educational systems, see [1])

4. Assimilative, Information Processing, Communicative, Productive, Experiential, Adaptive (from Martin Oliver and Gráinne Conole)

5. Guidance & Support, Communication & Collaboration, Reflection & Demonstration, Content & Activities (from Gráinne Conole)

6. Considered in terms of "Learning Power" (Ruth Deakin-Crick *et al.*)

7. Multiple intelligences (after Howard Gardner)

8. The associated "mental state" (after Mihaly Csíkszentmihályi; see picture)

Peer learning for one

Can you apply the ideas of peer learning on your own? In a certain sense, it's impossible, but somehow that never stops people from trying. We find a striking parallel between the paragogy principles and the 5 Elements of Effective Thinking proposed by Edward Burger and Michael Starbird in a recent book [2]. It's a nice short book and worth a read. Here, we will just quote the titles of the main chapters:

An Overview

CHALLENGE VS. SKILL. By w:User:Oliverbeatson (w:File:Challenge vs skill.jpg) [Public domain]

1. Quintessence, Engaging Change: Transform Yourself

2. Earth, Grounding Your Thinking: Understanding Deeply

3. Air, Creating Questions out of Thin Air: Be your own Socrates

4. Water, Seeing the Flow of Ideas: Look Back, Look Forward

5. Fire, Igniting Insights through Mistakes: Fail to Succeed

We think that "thinking" is often most effective when it's done with others, and this is something that Burger and Starbird don't give much attention. Nevertheless, even when you find yourself on your own in the midst of that challenging DIY project, you can use the techniques of peer learning to understand yourself as a growing, changing part of a shared context in motion. This can contribute to an effective and adaptive outlook on life.

We invite you to approach this book as a "peer learner" – and we hope the techniques we've introduced here will serve you well in the world at large. The book, in part, documents the growth of our subject as it moved from a critical and basically normative view to a richer descriptive theory, rooted in a collection strategies for doing emergent design. It's been fun – and worthwhile (if also frustrating at times) – working on it. We sincerely hope you enjoy the rest of the book, but don't be sparing with your criticism and creative ideas! You'll find some further reflections on these matters in the sections on peeragogical assessment.

References

1. Corneli, J., and Mikroyannidis, A. (2012). Crowdsourcing education on the Web: a role-based analysis of online learning communities, in Alexandra Okada, Teresa Conolly, and Peter Scott (eds.), Collaborative Learning 2.0: Open Educational Resources, IGI Global.

2. Burger, E. and Starbird, M. (2013). The 5 Elements of Effective Thinking, Princeton University Press.

Part III

Motivation

CHAPTER 5

WHY WE'RE DOING THIS

Participants must bring self-knowledge and no small measure of honesty to the peer-learning project in order to accurately enunciate their motivations. If everyone in your peer learning project asks "What brings me here?" "How can I contribute?" and "How can I contribute more effectively?" things will really start percolating. Test this suggestion by asking these questions yourself and taking action on the answers!

The primary motivators reported by participants in the Peeragogy project include:

1. Acquisition of training or support in a topic or field;

2. Building relationships with interesting people;

3. Finding professional opportunities through other participants;

4. Creating or bolstering a personal network;

5. More organized and rational thinking through dialog and debate;

6. Feedback about their own performance and understanding of the topic.

We've seen that different motivations can affect the vitality of the peeragogical process and the end result for the individual participant. And different participants definitely have different motivations, and the differences can be surprising: for instance, if you're motivated by social image, you may not be so interested in reciprocity, and vice versa [1]. Motivations come with associated risks. For example, one may be reluctant to mention business aspirations in a volunteer context for fear of seeming greedy or commercial. Whether or not potential peeragogues eventually decide to take on the risk depends on various factors. Actions that typify inappropriate behavior in one culture might represent desirable behavior in another. Motivations often come out of the closet through conflict; for example, when one learner feels offended or embarrassed by the actions of another.

> **Philip Spalding**: *"The idea of visiting a garden together in a group to learn the names of flowers might have been the original intention for forming a Garden Group. The social aspect of having a day out might be goal of the people participating."*

"What's my motivation?"

Example: Peeragogy editor Charlotte Pierce

Basically, I'm here because as an early adopter and admitted gadget freak, I find it fun and rewarding to explore new technologies and topics that I feel have a practical or exciting application. But I have some some other motivations that subtly co-exist alongside my eagerness to explore and learn.

Howard Rheingold's reputation as an innovator and internet pioneer got my attention when he announced his Think-Know Tools course on Facebook in 2012. I had known of Howard from the 1990's when I was a member of The WELL (Whole Earth 'Lectronic Link). I was curious to see what Howard was up to, so I signed onto the wiki site, paid my $300, and took the course starting in October.

Looking back, I realize we were practicing Peeragogy throughout the TKT course, though at the time I hardly knew peer learning from a pickle. In late November, missing the camaraderie and challenge of TKT, I stepped over to check out the *Peeragogy Handbook*.

Which brings me to motivations in signing on to Peeragogy. Since Howard and several Think-Know Tools co-learners were already dedicating their time here and their work looked innovative and exciting, I suspected they might be onto something that I wanted to be a part of. Plus, my brain was primed by the TKT experience. "What if a diverse group of people could learn a subject with little or no cost and not a lot of barriers to entry," I thought. "What if their own experience qualified them to join, contribute, and learn."

I also thought there might be a chance to meet some potential business partners or clients there - but if not, the experience looked rewarding and fun enough for me to take the risk of no direct remuneration. There was no up front cost to me, and a wealth of knowledge to gain as a part of something new and exciting. These are always big draws for me. I wanted to be in on it, and nobody was telling me I couldn't!

My projections proved correct. The participants already on board were gracious in welcoming me to Peeragogy, patient in getting me up to speed, and persistent in coaxing me into using the tools central to the project. I connected, learned, grew, and contributed. Now I'm on the brink of starting a peer learning project of my own in my publishing organization, IPNE.org. Stay tuned!

Example: Cafes, schools, workshops

Suppose we wanted to make Peeragogy into a model that can be used in schools, libraries, and so forth, worldwide - and, in fact we do! How can we bring the basic Peeragogy motivations to bear, and make a resource, plan of action, and process that other people can connect with? In brief, how do we build peer learning into the curriculum, providing new insight from the safety of the existing structure?

One concrete way to implement these broad aims would be to make a peeragogy-oriented *development* project whose goal is to set up a system of internet cafes, schools, or workshops in places like China or Africa, where people could go to collaborate on work or to learn technical subjects. Students could learn on the job. It seems reasonable to think that investors could make a reasonable profit through "franchises," hardware sales, and so forth – and obviously making money is a motivation that most people can relate to.

In developing such a project, we would want to learn from other similar projects that already exist. For example, in Chicago, State Farm Insurance has created a space called the "NEXT DOOR CAFE" that runs community events. One of their offerings is free financial coaching, with the explicit agreement that the issues you discuss return to State Farm as market research.

> **State Farm**: "Free? Really. Yes, because we're experimenting. We want to learn what people really want. Then, we'll shoot those wants back to the Farm. We help you. You help us innovate. We're all smarter for it. We think it's a win-win."

Thus, Next Door Cafe forms part of a system to exploit the side-effects of interpersonal interactions to create a system that learns. A peer learning example from the opposite side of the world started in a slum next to New Delhi where Sugata Mitra gave children a computer and they self organized into a learning community and taught themselves how to use the machine and much more.

Sugata Mitra: I think what we need to look at is we need to look at learning as the product of educational self-organization. If you allow the educational process to self-organize, then learning emerges. It's not about making learning happen. It's about letting it happen.

In 2014, we're going to try a somewhat similar experiment: Can we build a "Peeragogy Accelerator" for a half-dozen peer learning projects, each of which defines their own metrics for success, but who come together to offer support and guidance, using the *Peeragogy Handbook* as a resource?

Reference

1. Jérôme Hergueux (2013). Cooperation in a Peer Production Economy: Experimental Evidence from Wikipedia, talk presented at the Berkman Center for Internet and Society.

2. Hugo Mercier and Dan Sperber (2011). Why do humans reason? Arguments for an argumentative theory, *Behavioral and Brain Sciences*, 34, 57-111

CHAPTER 6

CASE STUDY: 5PH1NX

5PH1NX: 5tudent Peer Heuristic for 1Nformation Xchange - we think of it as a "curiously trans-media" use case in peeragogical assessment.

Author: David Preston

Over the last several decades technology has driven massive shifts in the way we communicate and collaborate. Information technology, socioeconomic trends, an increasingly complex and uncertain future, and school's failed brand are contributing factors in an emerging discourse that seeks to align learning with our rapidly changing culture.

Open Source Learning and Peeragogy, two emerging theoretical frameworks in this discourse, leverage end-to-end user principles of communication technology to facilitate peers learning together and teaching each other. In both traditional and liminal learning communities, one of the major points of contact between education and societal culture is the purposeful use of assessment. The processes of giving, receiving, and applying constructive critique makes learners better thinkers, innovators, motivators, collaborators, coworkers, friends, relatives, spouses, teammates, and neighbors. Implementing peer-based assessment can be problematic in schooling institutions where evaluative authority is traditionally conflated with hierarchical authority, and where economic and political influences have focused attention on summative, quantitative, standardized measurement of learning and intelligence.

This is the story of how one learning community is adopting Open Source Learning and Peeragogical principles to decentralize and enrich the assessment process.

Aldous Huxley: Knowledge is acquired when we succeed in fitting a new experience into the system of concepts based upon our old experiences. Understanding comes when we liberate ourselves from the old and so make possible a direct, unmediated contact with the new, the mystery, moment by moment, of our existence.

Enter 5PH1NX

On Monday, April 2, 2011, students in three English classes at a California public high school discovered anomalies in the day's entry on their course blog. (Reminder: not so long ago this sentence would have been rightly interpreted as being science fiction.) The date was wrong and the journal topic was this:

> In The Principles of Psychology (1890), William James wrote, "The faculty of voluntarily bringing back a wandering attention, over and over again, is the very root of judgment, character and will. No one is *compos sui* if he have it not. An education which should improve this faculty would be the education par excellence." How have your experiences in this course helped you focus your attention? What do you still need to work on? What elements of the following text (from Haruki Murakami's *1Q84*) draw your attention and help you construct meaning? The driver nodded and took the money. "Would you like a receipt?" "No need. And keep the change." "Thanks very much," he said. "Be careful, it looks windy out there. Don't slip." "I'll be careful," Aomame said. "And also," the driver said, facing the mirror, "please remember: things are not what they seem." Things are not what they seem,

Case Study: 5PH1NX

Aomame repeated mentally. "What do you mean by that?" she asked with knitted brows. The driver chose his words carefully: "It's just that you're about to do something out of the ordinary. Am I right? People do not ordinarily climb down the emergency stairs of the Metropolitan Expressway in the middle of the day–especially women." "I suppose you're right." "Right. And after you do something like that, the everyday look of things might seem to change a little. Things may look *different* to you than they did before. I've had that experience myself. But don't let appearances fool you. There's always only one reality."

Find the jokers

The jokers were real [4] and hidden (without much intent to conceal) around the classroom and in students' journals. Students found them and asked questions about the letters in bold; the questions went unanswered. Some thought it was just another of their teacher's wild hair ideas. Although they didn't know it yet they were playing the liminal role that Oedipus originated in mythology. Solving the riddle would enable them to usher out an old way of thinking and introduce the new. The old way: An authority figure sets the rules, packages the information for a passive audience, and unilaterally evaluates each learner's performance. In that context, peeragogical assessment might be introduced with a theoretical framework, a rubric, and a lesson plan with input, checks for understanding, and guided practice as a foundation for independent work. The new way: In Open Source Learning the learner pursues a path of inquiry within communities that function as end-to-end user networks. Each individual begins her learning with a question and pursues answers through an interdisciplinary course of study that emphasizes multiple modalities and the five Fs: mental Fitness, physical Fitness, spiritual Fitness, civic Fitness, and technological Fitness. Learners collaborate with mentors and receive feedback from experts, community-based peers, and the public. They are the heroes of learning journeys. Heroes don't respond to syllabi. They respond to calls to adventure. Open Source Learning prepares students for the unforeseen. By the time they met the 5PH1NX students had learned about habits of mind, operating schema, digital culture and community, self-expression, collaboration, free play, autonomy, confidence/trust/risk, and resilience. These ideas had been reinforced through nonfiction articles and literary selections such as Montaigne's Essays, Plato's Allegory of the Cave, Bukowski's Laughing Heart, Shakespeare's Hamlet, Sartre's No Exit and others. The first poem assigned in the course was Bukowski's "Laughing Heart?": *The Gods will offer you chances. Know them. Take them.* So it is with knowledge and understanding. Today we are presented with an overwhelming, unprecedented quantity and variety of data in our physical and virtual lives; to cope we must improve the ways we seek, select, curate, analyze, evaluate, and act on information. On the back of each Joker card was a QR code that linked to a blog page with riddles and clues to a search. At this point students realized they were playing a game. A tab on the blog page labeled "The Law" laid out the rules of engagement:

Case Study: 5PH1NX

This is The Law

1. You cannot "obey" or "break" The Law. You can only make good decisions or bad decisions.
2. Good decisions lead to positive outcomes.
3. Bad decisions lead to suffering.
4. Success requires humanity.
5. "For the strength of the Pack is the Wolf, and the strength of the Wolf is the Pack." -Rudyard Kipling
6. "The Way of the sage is to act but not to compete." -Lao Tzu
7. Be honorable.
8. Have fun.
9. Question.
10. *Sapere aude.*

This is The Law. After a second set of on-campus and blog quests, students noticed a shift in 5PH1NX. A couple of weeks before the first clue was published, during a Socratic seminar on Derrida's concept of Free Play, a student said, "We learn best when adults take away the crutches and there is no safety net."? The quote was used in the next clue; students began to realize that the game was not pre-determined. 5PH1NX was evolving in response to their contributions. This is a manifestation of the hackneyed writing cliché: show, don't tell. The student's comment was a call to action. The Feats of Wisdom were designed to engage learners over a vacation break in fun, collaborative, social media-friendly missions that required engagement in the community, expansion of their personal learning networks, and documentation on their blogs. For example:

FEAT #1

Buy a ticket to "The Hunger Games" (or any other movie that's likely to draw a large, young, rowdy audience). Before the lights dim and the trailers begin, walk to the screen, turn to the audience, and in a loud, clear voice, recite the "To be, or not to be..." soliloquy from Hamlet (don't worry if you make a couple mistakes, just be sure you make it all the way to, "Be all my sins remembered."). CAPTURE THE EVENT ON VIDEO & POST IT TO YOUR BLOG. Students had been using the Internet without an Acceptable Use Policy all year; such policies are one-to-many artifacts of a central authority and far weaker than community norms. So rather than introduce "rules" 5PH1NX simply provided a reminder of the client-side responsibility.

The Emergence of Peeragogical Assessment

The third page on the Feats of Wisdom blog was entitled *Identifying and Rewarding Greatness*, where learners were greeted with the following paragraph:

> If you see something that was done with love, that pushed the boundaries, set the standard, broke the mold, pushed the envelope, raised the bar, blew the doors off, or rocked in some previously unspecified way, please bring it to the attention of the tribe by posting a link to it [here].

No one did. Instead, they started doing something more effective. They started building. One student hacked the entire game and then created her own version. Other students began to consider the implications for identifying and rewarding greatness. They realized that one teacher couldn't possibly observe how 96 students were working over vacation out in the community and online to accomplish the Feats of Wisdom. In order to get credit for their efforts they would have to curate and share their work-process and product. They also realized that the same logic applied to learning and coursework in general; after all, even the most engaged, conscientious teacher only sees a high school or college student a few hours a week, under relatively artificial conditions. The learner presumably spends her whole life in the company of her own brain. Who is the more qualified reporting authority?

With these thoughts in mind students created *Project Infinity*, a peer-to-peer assessment platform through which students could independently assign value to the thoughts and activities they deemed worthy. Because the 2011-12 5PH1NX was a three-week exercise in gamification, *Project Infinity* quickly evolved to include collaborative working groups and coursework. This was learner-centered Peeragogical assessment in action; learners identified a need and an opportunity, they built a tool for the purpose, they managed it themselves, and they leveraged it in a meaningful way to support student achievement in the core curriculum.

Project Infinity 2 & Implications for the Future

Alumni from the Class of 2012 felt such a strong positive connection to their experience in Open Source Learning and Peeragogical assessment that they built a version for the Class of 2013. They created *Project Infinity2* with enhanced functionality. They asked the teacher to embed an associated Twitter feed on the course blog, then came to classes to speak with current students about their experiences. Everyone thought the Class of 2013 would stand on the shoulders of giants and adopt the platform with similar enthusiasm.

They were wrong. Students understood the concept and politely contributed suggestions for credit, but it quickly became evident that they weren't enthusiastic. Submissions decreased and finally the *Project Infinity2* Twitter feed disappeared from the course blog. Learners' blogs and project work suggested that they were mastering the core curriculum and meta concepts, and they appeared generally excited about Open Source Learning overall. So why weren't they more excited about the idea of assessing themselves and each other? Because *Project Infinity2* wasn't theirs. They didn't get to build it. It was handed to them in the same way that a syllabus is handed to them. No matter how innovative or effective it might be, *Project Infinity2* was just another tool designed by someone else to get students to do something they weren't sure they wanted or needed to do in the first place. Timing may also be a factor. Last year's students didn't meet 5PH1NX until the first week in April, well into the spring semester.

This year's cohort started everything faster and met 5PH1NX in November. In January they understood the true potential of their situation started to take the reins. As students realized what was happening with the clues and QR codes they approached the teacher and last year's alumni with a request: "Let Us In." They don't just want to design learning materials or creatively demonstrate mastery, they want to chart their own course and build the vehicles for taking the trip. Alumni and students are becoming Virtual TAs who will start the formal peer-to-peer advising and grading process. In the Spring Semester all students will be asked to prepare a statement of goals and intentions, and they will be informed that the traditional teacher will be responsible for no more than 30% of their grade. The rest will come from a community of peers, experts and members of the public. On Tuesday of Finals Week, 5PH1NX went from five players to two hundred. Sophomores and freshman have jumped into the fray and hacked/solved one of the blog clues before seniors did. Members of the Open Source Learning cohort have also identified opportunities to enrich and expand 5PH1NX. A series of conversations about in-person retreats and the alumni community led to students wanting to create a massively multiple player learning cohort. Imagine 50,000-100,000 learners collaborating and sharing information on a quest to pass an exam by solving a puzzle that leads them to a "Learning Man Festival" that takes place over Summer break.

When 5PH1NX players return from Winter Break in January they will transform their roles relative to the game and the course. Several have already shared "AHA!" moments in which they discovered ways to share ideas and encourage collaboration and peer assessment. They have identified Virtual Teaching Assistant candidates, who will be coached by alumni, and they have plans to provide peer-based assessment for their online work. They are also now actively engaged in taking more control over the collaboration process itself. On the last day of the semester, a post-finals throwaway day of 30-minute class sessions that adminis-

Case Study: 5PH1NX

trators put on the calendar to collect Average Daily Attendance money, hardly anyone came to campus. But Open Source Learning students were all there. They have separated the experience of learning from the temporal, spatial, and cultural constraints of school. They understand how democracy works: those who participate make the decisions. No one knows how this ends, but the outcome of Peeragogical assessment is not a score; it is learners who demonstrate their thinking progress and mastery through social production and peer-based critique. This community's approach to learning and assessment has prepared its members for a complex and uncertain future by moving them from a world of probability to a world of possibility. As one student put it in a video entitled "We Are Superman," "What we are doing now may seem small, but we are part of something so much bigger than we think. What does this prove? It proves everything; it proves that it's possible."

Background

A world in which work looks like what's described in the PSFK think tank's FUTURE OF WORK REPORT 2013 requires a new learning environment.

The problem is that tools and strategies such as MOOCs, videos, virtual environments, and games are only as good as the contexts in which they are used. Even the most adept practitioners quickly discover that pressing emerging technology and culture into the shape of yesterday's curricular and instructional models amounts to little more than Skinner's Box 2.0. So what is to be done? How can we use emerging tools and culture to deliver such an amazing individual and collaborative experience that it shatters expectations and helps students forget they're in school long enough to fall in love with learning again?

Education in the Information Age should enable learners to find, analyze, evaluate, curate, and act on the best available information. Pursuing an interdisciplinary path of inquiry in an interest-based community doesn't just facilitate the acquisition of factual knowledge (which has a limited half-life). The process brings learners closer to understanding their own habits of mind and gives them practice and an identity in the culture they'll be expected to join after they graduate. This requires new literacies and a curriculum that emphasizes mental fitness, physical fitness, spiritual fitness, civic fitness, and technological fitness.

Models of assessment that emphasize self-directed and collaborative Peeragogical principles enrich the learning experience and accelerate and amplify deep understanding. Because these approaches are pull-based and generate tens of thousands of multi- or trans-media data points per learner, they also generate multi-dimensional portraits of learner development and provide feedback that goes far beyond strengths and weaknesses in content retention. The long-term benefit is exponential. Learners who can intentionally direct their own concentration are empowered far beyond knowledge acquisition or skill mastery. They become more effective thinkers and – because they are invested – more caring people. This learning experience is of their own making: it isn't business, it's personal. The inspiration to recreate the process for themselves and for others is the wellspring of the lifelong learner.

As Benjamin Disraeli put it, "In general the most successful man in life is the man who has the best information." It is a widely accepted truism in business that better data leads to better decisions. We now have the ability to generate, aggregate, analyze, and evaluate much richer data sets that can help us learn more about helping each other learn. Sharing richer data in different ways will have the same game changing effect in learning that it has in professional sports and investment banking.

Self-directed, collaborative assessment generates an unprecedented quantity and variety of data that illuminates aspects of learning, instruction, and overall systemic efficacy. Even a quick look at readily available freeware metrics, blog/social media content, and time stamps can provide valuable insight into an individual's working process and differentiate learners in a network.

In the larger scheme of things, Peeragogical assessment provides direct access to and practice in the culture learners will be expected to join when they complete their course of study.

CASE STUDY: 5PH1NX 59

Collaboration, delegation, facilitating conversations, and other highly valued skills are developed in plain view, where progress can be critiqued and validated by peers, experts and the public.

But tall trees don't grow by themselves in the desert. Peeragogical innovation can be challenging in organizational cultures that prioritize control and standardization; as Senge *et al.* have observed, the system doesn't evaluate quality when dealing with the unfamiliar, it just pushes back. In schools this is so typical that it doesn't merit comment in traditional media. The world notices when Syria goes dark, but in school, restricted online access is business as usual.

Cultural constraints can make early adopters in technology-based Peeragogy seem like Promethean risk-takers. Whenever the author gives a talk or an interview, someone asks if he's in trouble.

Learners are not fooled by the rhetoric of in loco parentis or vision statements that emphasize "safe, nurturing learning environments." With notable exceptions, today's school leaders do not know as much about technology as the young people for whom they assume responsibility. Still, learners understand survival: they are fighting in unfavorable terrain against an enemy of great power. Innovating is impossible, and even loudly criticizing school or advocating for change is a risk. As a result many do just enough to satisfy requirements without getting involved enough to attract attention. Some have also internalized the critical voices of authority or the failure of the formal experience as evidence of their own inability: "I'm just not good at math."

How do we know when we're really good at something? Standardized testing feedback doesn't help learners improve. Most of us don't have a natural talent for offering or accepting criticism. And yet, as Wole Soyinka put it, "The greatest threat to freedom is the absence of criticism."? Peeragogical interaction requires refining relational and topical critique, as well as skills in other "meta" literacies, including but not limited to critical thinking, collaboration, conflict resolution, decision-making, mindfulness, patience and compassion.

Interpersonal learning skills are undervalued in today's

schooling paradigm. Consequently there is an operational lack of incentive for teachers and learners to devote time and energy, particularly when it carries a perceived cost in achievement on tests that determine financial allocations and job security. In recent years there has been increasing pressure to tie teacher compensation, performance evaluation, and job status directly to student performance on standardized tests.

Some educators are introducing peer-to-peer network language and even introducing peer-based assessment. But the contracts, syllabi and letters to students typically stink of *the old way*. These one-to-many documents are presented by agents of the institution endowed with the power to reward or punish. To many students this does not represent a choice or a real opportunity to hack the learning experience. They suspect manipulation, and they wait for the other shoe to drop. Learners also don't like to be told they're free while being forced to operate within tight constraints. Consider this likely reaction to a policy that is highly regarded in the field:

> "Students may choose to reblog their work in a public place or on their own blogs, but do so at their own risk."
>
> *What? Did I read that correctly?*
>
> "Students may choose to reblog their work in a public place or on their own blogs, but do so at their own risk."
>
> *Risk? What risk? The risk of possibly helping someone understand something that they didn't before, or get a different opinion than the one they had before? Someone please help me make sense of this.*

To effectively adopt Peeragogical assessment in the schooling context, the community must construct a new understanding of how the members in a network relate to one another independent of their roles in the surrounding social or hierarchical systems.

Case Study: 5PH1NX

This requires trust, which in school requires significant suspension of disbelief, which – and this is the hard part – requires actual substantive, structural change in the learning transaction. This is the defining characteristic of Open Source Learning: as the network grows, changes composition, and changes purpose, it also changes the direction and content of the learning experience. Every network member can introduce new ideas, ask questions, and contribute resources than refine and redirect the process.

This isn't easy. A member in this network must forget what she knows about school in order to test the boundaries of learning that shape her relationship to content, peers, and expert sources of information and feedback. This is how the cogs in the machine become the liminal heroes who redesign it. Having rejected the old way, they must now create the rituals that will come to define the new. They are following in the path of Oedipus, who took on the inscrutable and intimidating Sphinx, solved the riddle that had killed others who tried, and ushered out the old belief systems to pave the way for the Gods of Olympus. Imagine, what if Oedipus had the Internet.

Part IV

Peeragogy in Practice

CHAPTER 7

THINKING ABOUT PATTERNS

Although a grounding in learning theory helps inform peer learning projects, Peeragogy, at its core, comes to life in applied practice. Even before convening a group for your peer learning project, you will want to take a look over the patterns we have collected here. You will likely return here many times as your project develops.

What is a pattern?

A pattern is anything that has a repeated effect. In the context of peeragogy, the practice is to repeat processes and interactions that advance the learning mission. Frequent occurrences that are not desirable are called anti-patterns!

> **Christopher Alexander**: "Each pattern describes a problems which occurs over and over again in our environment, and then describes the core of the solution to that problem, in a way that you can use this solution a million times over, without ever doing it the same way twice." [1]

Patterns provide a framework that can be applied to similar issues but may be metaphorically solved in different ways, sometimes in real world or face to face events and other times in digital space. Outside of Alexander's own work in architecture, one the first groups to adopt a design pattern way of thinking about things were computer programmers. Writing in the foreward to Richard P. Gabriel's *Patterns of Software*, Alexander emphasizes that the key question to ask about any design approach is: does it help us build better?

> **Christopher Alexander**: "What is the Chartres of programming? What task is at a high enough level to inspire people writing programs, to reach for the stars?" [2]

We think that Peeragogy stands a good chance of being a "killer app" for pattern-based design. Learning bridges physical and virtual worlds all the time. And, in fact, a *Network of Learning* was the 18th pattern that Christopher Alexander introduced in his book, *A Pattern Language*.

> **Christopher Alexander**: "Work in piecemeal ways to decentralize the process of learning and enrich it through contact with many places and people all over the city: workshops, teachers at home or walking through the city, professionals willing to take on the young as helpers, older children teaching younger children, museums, youth groups travelling, scholarly seminars, industrial workshops, old people, and so on." [1]

Peeragogy can help to extend and enrich this network, and, as we shall see, patterns can be used by those involved to do ongoing "emergent" design, not only by building new structures, but by adapting and improving our catalog of patterns as we go.

Patterns of peeragogy

Here is our index of the main patterns we've found so far (described in more detail after the jump):

- **Wrapper** - Front end appearance to participants. Consolidate and summarize.

- **Discerning a pattern** - Found a pattern? Give it a title and record an example. (Woah, meta!)

- **Polling for ideas** - Invite brainstorming, collecting ideas, questions, and solutions.

- **Creating a guide** - Overviews expose the lay of the land. Collecting content and stories.

- **Newcomer** - Create a guide for "beginner's mind" and help avoid need to introduce new members each "meeting."

- **Roadmap** - Plans for future work, direction towards a goal, dynamic

- **Roles** - Specialize and mix it up. Play to participants strengths and skills.

- **Project focus** - Lightbulb moment: Most specific projects involve learning!

- **Carrying capacity** - Know your limits, find ways to get other people involved.

- **Heartbeat** - The "heartbeat" of the group keeps energy flowing.

- **Moderation** - When leaders step back, dynamics can improve; moderator serves as champion and editor.

- **Use or make?** - Repurposing, tinkering, or creating from scratch?

We'll introduce three additional patterns in the chapter on researching peeragogy.

Anti-patterns for Peeragogy

And some "anti-patterns" (things to avoid if possible):

- **Isolation** - A tale of silos, holes, and not-invented-here.

- **Magical thinking** - "One meeting will (not) change everything!"

- **Messy with Lurkers** - What happens when joining is low-cost and completion is low-benefit.

- **Misunderstanding Power** - The workload is almost never evenly distributed.

- **Navel Gazing** - "I have this really great idea..."

- **Stasis** - What is the driver behind open source, commons-oriented collaborative projects? (Because, let's face it, it doesn't always work.)

- **Stuck at the level of weak ties** - Can we deepen the connection?

What is a use case?

A use case describes someone (or something) who uses a given system or tool to achieve a goal. A use case can include a title, a summary of the problem, an actor, and a success scenario. Additional features can be added, such as alternate interactions or choices that lead to a variation on the result.

The use case considers a given persona (a characteristic role) in a given situation and shows how they works on a project/problem and how their process of work is resolved into a solution or solutions. Some activities do not have a single solution – these are often referred to as "Wicked Problems." With detailed bookkeeping effort, recorded processes can be standardized into use cases that can then be employed directly or modified to fit the context of the activity at hand. In short, they are a lot like design patterns, which they may contain in hidden or explicit form. Use cases are presented in vignettes that appear throughout the book (like the one at the end of this section).

A peeragogy pattern language

By looking at how patterns combine in real and hypothetical use cases, you can start to identify a *pattern language* that can be used in your projects. We can get a simplified view of these connections with the following diagram. It's important to clarify that everyone doesn't do it the same way. Here, the *Roadmap*

Thinking about patterns 69

is given a central position, but some peer learning projects will forego making a specific, detailed plan; their plan is just to see what develops. You can see here how peeragogy patterns often break down further into individual micro-steps: we'll say more about that shortly.

```
                        Do you know the answer
                                |
                          Use or make?
         Change focus           |
                  \          Assess
 Give it a rest — Carrying Capacity                      Ask yourself: why is it hard?
               \     \         |                       /
          Heartbeat – Cooperate – Roadmap – Convene – A specific project – Creating a guide
               /     /         |                                         \
          Moderation           Organize                                Find an analogy
      Ask for help  \            |
                 Polling for ideas   Divide
                               Roles
                         Wrapper /    \ Mentor
                              Newcomer
```

The subsequent main sections of this book – *Convene*, *Organize*, *Cooperate* and *Assess* – represent big clusters of patterns that are likely to come up time and again in various projects. We can think of these as East, South, West, and North in the diagram above. You are of course encouraged to invent your own patterns and to connect them in new ways. Each project has a unique design, and it's own unique way in which things play out in practice. What we've put together here is a starter kit.

> **Christopher Alexander**: These ideas—patterns—are hardly more than glimpses of a much deeper level of structure, and is ultimately within this deeper level of structure, that the origin of life occurs. [2]

Patterns and Problem Solving

Ten potentially useful things to do when you're solving a problem are described by the computer scientist Marvin Minsky in a series of MEMOS written for the One Laptop Per Child project. We can sum them up visually with the following diagram:

We can also see some interesting connections between these intuitive problem solving heuristics and peeragogy patterns listed

| simplify | change focus | change description | divide | find an analogy |

| ask for help | do you know the answer? | give it a rest | what do experts do? | why is it hard? |

above. This can help illustrate further connections between the patterns, and some of the ways that groups can apply them to solve real-world problem. To elaborate briefly:

- Simplify things for **Newcomers**. We don't expect a newcomer to enter at full speed.

- Use a **Roadmap** to guide us from one phase to another, while the project's central **Heartbeat** helps us attend to the central focus.

- Announce changes through a **Wrapper** who describes the new status or direction of the project. For the Peeragogy project, that often meant summing up the high points that we saw over a given period of time.

- We divide work up not only horizontally among different **Roles**, but also temporally by using the **Roadmap**. Someone who is moving ahead with the Roadmap is likely to be working at the leading edge.

- When we find an analogy, we are basically **Creating a Guide** for thinking about something. This can be used as a form of "exploration," as we look at how one form of engagement may or may not map onto other forms of engagement.

- When we ask for help, we may avail ourselves of some **Moderation** service that will decide how to deal with our request. One simple way to ask for help is **Polling for Ideas**. Obviously once we start to get help, we're working in a regime of "collaborative effort".

- If you know the answer, then you may be able to reuse it (which is the basic idea described in **Use or Make**.

- It is important to give it a rest so as not to over-exhaust oneself, busting one's own **Carrying Capacity**, or, alternatively, overwhelming the group.

- It seems that one of the things that experts are good at is **Discerning a Pattern**. This allows them to simplify their processing.

- Finally, again, if we know why it is hard, then we may be able to **Create a Guide** that will help get around, or at least better cope with, the difficulty.

References

1. Alexander, Christopher, Ishikawa, Sara, and Silverstein, Murray, *A Pattern Language: Towns, Buildings, and, Construction*, New York: Oxford University Press, 1977.

2. Gabriel, Richard P. PATTERNS OF SOFTWARE, New York: Oxford University Press, 1996. (Includes a forward by Christopher Alexander.)

CHAPTER 8

PATTERNS

Wrapper

Early on, active peeragogue Charlie Danoff SUGGESTED that someone take on the "wrapper role" – do a weekly pre/post wrap, so that new users would know the status the project is at any given point in time. The project's WIKI PAGE also serves as another sort of "wrapper". We check the public summaries of the project from time to time to make sure that they accurately represent the facts on the ground. Note that in its various forms, the "wrapper role" plays an important integrative function.

According to the theory proposed by Yochai Benkler, for free/open "commons-based" projects to work, it is vital to have both (1) the ability to contribute small pieces; (2) something that stitches those pieces together [1]. In the first year of the Peeragogy project, the "Weekly Roundup" by Christopher Tillman Neal served to engage and re-engage members. Peeragogues began to eager watched for the weekly reports to see if our teams or our names had been mentioned. When there was a holiday or break, Chris would announce the hiatus, to keep the flow going.

In the second year of the project, we didn't routinely publish summaries of progress, and instead, we've assumed that interested parties will stay tuned on Google+. Nevertheless, we maintain internal and external summaries, ranging from agendas to press releases to quick-start guides. Regular meetings provide an alternative way to stay up to date: see the Heartbeat pattern.

Reference

1. Benkler, Y. (2002). Coase's Penguin, or Linux and the Nature of the Firm, *Yale Law Journal* 112, pp. 369-446.

Discerning a Pattern

Discerning patterns helps us build our vocabulary or repertoire for peer-learning projects. As a very simple example, in building a peer learning profile, a participant might identify an interest such as organic gardening. We begin to notice that this is a pattern when it repeats – when organic gardening is frequently listed among the interests listed by participants in their self-introductions. The classic example of an architectural pattern is *"A place to wait"* —a type of space found in many architectural and urban design projects. Once a pattern is detected, give it a title and write down how the pattern works. For example, what does this pattern say about the self-selection process of the group? Without jumping to conclusions, consider that an interest in organic gardening, for example, might indicate the participants are oriented to cooperation, personal health, or environmental activism. How does the pattern relate to other patterns already listed in this catalog?

Polling for Ideas

... and then Howard said: "At the beginning, until we all know the ropes well enough to understand when to create a new discussion forum topic and when to add to an existing one, let's talk in this topic thread about what else we want to discuss and I will start new topic threads when necessary." Polling for Ideas can happen at many junctures in a peer learning experience. We could poll for ideas like "what's missing?", "who might like to join our group?", and "what are the right tools and resources for us to use at this point?"

Creating a Guide

Meaning-carrying tools, like handbooks or maps, can help people use an idea. In particular, when the idea or system is only

Patterns

"newly discovered", the associated meanings may not be well understood (indeed they may not have been created). In such a case, the process of creating the guide can go hand-in-hand with figuring out how the system works. Thus, techniques of KNOWLEDGE CARTOGRAPHY and MEANING MAKING are useful for would-be guide creators. Even so, it is worth noting that "the map is not the territory," and map-making is only one facet of shared human activity. Collaboratively refining a pattern is itself an example of "Creating a Guide" - that is, a pattern description can be thought of as a "micro-map" of a specific activity.

Newcomer

Unless there is a new person to talk to, a lot of the "education stuff" we do could grow stale. Many of the patterns and use cases for peeragogy assume that there will be an audience or a new generation of learners - hence the drive to create a guide. Note that the newcomer and the wrapper may work together to make the project accessible. Even in the absence of actual newcomers, we're often try to look at things with a "beginner's mind."

Régis Barondeau: I joined this handbook project late, making me a "newcomer". When I started to catch up, I rapidly faced doubts: *Where do I start? How can I help? How will I make it, having to read more than 700 posts to catch up? What tools are we using ? How do I use them?* Etc. Although this project is amazingly interesting, catching the train while it already reached high speed can be an extreme sport. By taking care of newcomers, we might avoid loosing valuable contribuors because they don't know how and where to start, and keep our own project on track.

Charlotte Pierce: Joe was working a lot on the book, and I thought "this is interesting hard work, and he shouldn't have to do this alone." As a Peeragogy newcomer, I was kindly welcomed and mentored by Joe, Howard, Fabrizio, and others. I asked naive questions and was met with patient answers, guiding questions, and resource links. Concurrently, I bootstrapped myself into a position to contribute to the workflow by editing the live manuscript for consistency, style, and continuity.

Roadmap

It is very useful to have an up-to-date public roadmap for the project, a place where it can be discussed and maintained. This helps newcomers see where they can jump in. It also gives a sense of the accomplishments to date, and any major challenges that lie ahead. Remember, the Roadmap exists as an artifact with which to share current, but never complete, understanding of the space. Never stop learning!

Examples

In the Peeragogy project, once the book's outline became fairly mature, we could use it as a roadmap, by marking the sections that are "finished" (at least in draft), marking the sections where editing is currently taking place, and marking the stubs (possible starting points for future contributors). After this outline matured into a real table of contents, we started to look in other directions for ways to build on our successes to date, and started working on a roadmap for further development of the website and peeragogy project as a whole.

And also

Note that a shared roadmap is very similar to a Personal Learning Plan, or "paragogical profile". We've made some EXAMples of these as we got started working on the Free Technology Guild.

There is a certain roadmappiness to "presentation of self", and you can learn to use this well. For instance, when introducing yourself and your work to other people, you can focus on highlights like these:

- "What is the message behind what you're doing?"

- "How do you provide a model others can follow or improve upon?"

- "How can others get directly involved with your project?"

Roles

This may seem like an obvious one, but educational interactions tend to have a number of different roles associated with them. Consider that everything could bifurcate from the "autodidact":

1. Autodidact 2. Tutor-Tutee 3. Tutor-Tutee-Parent 4. Tutor-Tutee-Parent-Principal etc. —

Until we have bursars, librarians, technicians, janitors, editors of peer reviewed research journals, government policy makers, spin-off industrial ventures and partnerships, etc., all involved in Education. Even the autodidact may assume different roles at different points in time - sometimes making a library run, sometimes constructing a model, sometimes checking a proof. The decomposition of "learning" into different phases or polarities could be an endless theoretical task. For the moment, we just note that roles are often present "by default" at the start of a learning process, and that they may change as the process develops.

Focusing on a specific project

In the Jan. 2013 plenary session, as Independent Publishers of New England (IPNE) President Tordis Isselhardt quietly listened to a presentation about how we created the *Peeragogy Handbook*. During the Q&A, he spoke up, wondering if peer-learning effort in IPNE might be more likely to succeed if the organization's members "focused around a specific project." As this lightbulb illuminated the room, those of us attending the plenary session suggested that IPNE could focus the project by creating an "Independent Publishing Handbook." (Applause!)

In the course of creating the IPNE Handbook, peer learners would assemble resource repositories, exchange expertise, and collaboratively edit documents. To provide motivation and incentive to participate in "PeerPubU", members of the association will earn authorship credit for contributing articles, editor credit for working on the manuscript, and can spin off their own chapters as stand-alone, profit-making publications.

Carrying Capacity

> **Alvin Toffler**: If overstimulation at the sensory level increases the distortion with which we perceive reality, cognitive overstimulation interferes with our ability to 'think.'

At times, a facilitator or participant in the peer-learning enterprise may feel he or she is over-contributing – or, perhaps more likely, that others are under-contributing – or that someone else is railroading an idea or dominating the discussion. If this happens, take a step back and observe the dynamics of involvement. Ask questions and let others answer. Especially if you start to feel the symptoms of burnout, it's important that you find the level of engagement that allows you to participate at a level that is feasible for maintaining progress toward the project's goal. Lead by example – but make sure it's someplace you, and others, actually want to go! This could be a good time to revisit the group's roadmap and see if you can figure out and clarify to others what concrete goal you're working towards. Remember that you can also change the "landscape" by making it easier for other people to get involved – for example, by explaining what you're trying to do in a clear manner. Watch for opportunities to step back, watch, listen. Try to be mindful of phases when active or quiet involvement would be more helpful to the individual and the group. It's also helpful to let anyone who has taken on a facilitation role know if you're stepping back temporarily. Then, when the time is right, step back in and get to work!

Heartbeat

Without someone or something acting as the "heartbeat" for the group, energy may dissipate. In the "Collaborative Lesson Planning" course led by Charlie Danoff at P2PU, Charlie wrote individual emails to people who were signed up for the course and who had disappeared, or lurked but didn't participate. This kept a healthy number of the people in the group to reengage and make positive contributions. In more recent months, Charlotte Pierce has been running weekly meetings by Google Hangout to coordinate work on the *Peeragogy Handbook*. Not only have we gotten a lot of hands-on editorial work done this way, we've generated a tremendous amount of new material (both text and video footage) that is likely to find its way into future versions of the book.

Moderation

> **The Co-Intelligence Institute**: Why is a fishbowl more productive than debate? The small group conversations in the fishbowl tend to de-personalize the issue and reduce the stress level, making people's statements more cogent. Since people are talking with their fellow partisans, they get less caught up in wasteful adversarial games.

Participation in online forums tends to follow a "power law," with vastly unequal engagement. If you want to counteract this tendency, one possibility would simply be for the most active par-

19th century collage cards, care of NICK HAUS

ticipants to step back, and moderate how much they speak. This is related the the Carrying Capacity pattern and the Misunderstanding Power anti-pattern: check those out before you proceed. Occupy Wall Street used a related technique that they called the "PROGRESSIVE STACK." There are lots of other strategies to try.

Use or Make?

> "Praxis, a noble activity, is always one of use, as distinct from poesis which designates fabrication. Only the former, which plays and acts, but does not produce, is noble." [1] (p. 101)

There is a tension between "making stuff" (*poesis*) and "using stuff" (*praxis*). Peer *production*, as the name indicates, is about "making stuff." And making stuff can be fun. But we should also ask ourselves, how much new stuff do we really need? There's not a hard and fast answer to that. We should also consider how much "learning" is really "remix" – that is, re-use and recycling of other people's ideas and techniques. Understanding and negotiating the tension between reuse and creativity is the key to *the art of remix* or "paragogical praxis"!

Reference

1. Baudrillard, J. (1975). *The mirror of production.* Telos Press

CHAPTER 9

ANTIPATTERNS

Isolation

> **Félix Guattari**: Imagine a fenced field in which there are horses wearing adjustable blinkers, and let's say that the "coefficient of transversality" will be precisely the adjustment of the blinkers. If the horses are completely blind, a certain kind of traumatic encounter will be produced. As soon as the blinkers are opened, one can imagine that the horses will move about in a more harmonious way. (QUOTED BY ANDREW MURPHY, himself quoting Gary Genosko)

From a design point of view: we should be conscious of interfaces that are "too loud", and think about how that is compensated for by isolation of various forms. With a too-narrow focus, collaboration is impossible. However, with an overly-wide focus, things are chaotic in other ways (see Co-Learning: Messy with Lurkers).

This anti-pattern sometimes goes by the name *Not Invented Here*. Many projects that are ostensibly oriented towards "the commons" nevertheless want to funnel participants into "their way" of thinking about things. Be careful with that. Learning how to manage the uncertainty that comes with experimentation is part of what makes the postmodern organization tick! (See also: Navel Gazing.)

Magical thinking

While we could imagine an ideal information processing system that would (magically) come with all solutions pre-built, a more realistic approach recognizes that real problem solving always takes time and energy. For instance, if we "knew", 100%, how to do peeragogy, then we would not stand to learn very much by writing this handbook. Difficulties and tensions would be resolved "in advance". The relevant problem solving approach and associated "learning orientation" will depend on the task and resources at hand.

Magical thinking of the kind described above robs a context of its "process" or "motion". The more structure we have in advance, the more completely we fall back on "traditional" modes of doing things, and the less we stand to learn. It's also true that traditions and habits can serve a useful function: they can massively simplify and streamline, and adopting some healthy habits can free up time and energy, making learning possible [1]. But it's still going to take work. Time for a few deep breaths?

Reference

1. Dias-Ferreira, Eduardo, *et al.* "Chronic stress causes frontostriatal reorganization and affects decision-making." *Science* 325.5940 (2009): 621-625.

Messy with Lurkers

> **Gigi Johnson**: (1) Co-learning is Messy. It needs time, patience, confusion, re-forming, re-norming, re-storming, etc. Things go awry and part of norms needs to be how to realign. (2) Co-learning is a VERY different experience from traditional teacher-led learning in terms of time and completion. It is frustrating, so many people will lurk or just step in and out, the latter of which is very different from what is acceptable in traditonal learning. Online learning programs are painted with the brush now of an "unacceptable" 50% average non-completion rate. Stanford's MOOC AI class, which started out with +100,000 people, had 12% finish. If only 12% or 50% of my traditional class finished, I'd have a hard time getting next quarter's classes approved!

The second point is similar to the earlier Anti-pattern "Misunderstanding Power (Laws)". People have to join in order to try, and when joining is low-cost, and completion low-benefit, it is not surprising that many people will "dissipate" as the course progresses. The "messiness" of co-learning is interesting because it points to a sort of "internal dissipation", as contributors bring their multiple different backgrounds, interests, and communication styles to bear.

> **Tomlinson et al.**: More authors means more content, but also more words thrown away. Many of the words written by authors were deleted during the ongoing editing process. The sheer mass of deleted words might raise the question of whether authoring a paper in such a massively distributed fashion is efficient. [1]

If we were to describe this situation in traditional subject/object terms, we would say that peer production has a "low signal to noise ratio". However, it may be more appropriate (and constructive) to think of meanings as co-constructed as the process runs, and of messiness (or meaninglessness) as symptomatic, not of peer production *itself*, but of deficiencies or infelicities in shared meaning-making and "integrating" features.

Reference

1. Tomlinson, B., Ross, J., André, P., Baumer, E.P.S., Patterson, D.J., Corneli, J., Mahaux, M., Nobarany, S., Lazzari, M., Penzenstadler, B., Torrance, A.W., Callele, D.J., Olson, G.M., Silberman, M.S., Ständer, M., Palamedi, F.R., Salah, A., Morrill, E., Franch, X., Mueller, F., Kaye, J., Black, R.W., Cohn, M.L., Shih, P.C., Brewer, J., Goyal, N., Näkki, P., Huang, J., Baghaei, N., and Saper, C., MASSIVELY DISTRIBUTED AUTHORSHIP OF ACADEMIC PAPERS, *Proceedings of Alt.Chi, Austin Texas, May 5–10 2012* (10 page extended abstract), ACM, 2012,

Misunderstanding Power

> **Wikipedia**: Zipf's law states that given some corpus of natural language utterances, the frequency of any word is inversely proportional to its rank in the frequency table. Thus the most frequent word will occur approximately twice as often as the second most frequent word, three times as often as the third most frequent word, etc. [1]

Zipf's law (or other formulations of the same thing) govern the SIZE OF CITIES, and related formulations describe ENERGY USE: roughly speaking, an elephant has a lower metabolism than a mouse and is more "energy efficient". At that same link, we see the suggestion that creativity and other social network effects speed up as population grows! *The anti-pattern*: how many times have we been at a conference or workshop and heard someone say (or said ourselves) "wouldn't it be great if this energy could be sustained all year 'round?" Or in a classroom or peer production setting, wondered why it is that everyone does not participate equally. "Wouldn't it be great if we could increase participation?" But participation in a given population is going falls off according to *some* power law (see Introduction to Power Laws in THE UNCERTAINTY PRINCIPLE, VOLUME II, ISSUE 3). It would be a grand illusion to assume that everyone is coming from a similar place with regard to the various literacies and motivations that are conducive to participation. Furthermore, a "provisionist" attitude ("If we change our system we will equalize participation and access") simply will not work in general. Power laws are an inherent epiphenomenon of network flow. Certainly, if you can moderate the way the network is shaped, you can change the "exponent" – for example, by helping more people develop relevant literacies. But even so, "equality" remains a largely abstract notional. Note, as well, that participation in a given activity tends to fall off over time. Many people would like to write a hit song or a best selling novel or start a religion, etc., but few actually do, because it takes sustained effort over time. See the anti-pattern "Magical Thinking" for more on this. Our ability to develop new literacies is limited. Much as Paul Graham wrote about programming languages – programmers are typically "satisfied with whatever language they happen to use, because it dictates the way they think about programs" – so too are people often "satisfied" with their social environments, because these tend to dictate the way they think and act in life.

Reference

1. ZIPF'S LAW. (2013). In *Wikipedia, The Free Encyclopedia*.

2. Graham, P. (2001). BEATING THE AVERAGES.

Navel Gazing

The difficulty I am referring to breaks down like this:

1. Certainly we cannot get things done just by talking about them.

2. And yet, feedback *can* be useful, i.e., if there are mechanisms for responding to it in a useful fashion.

3. The associated *anti-pattern* is a special case of the prototypical Bateson DOUBLE BIND, "the father who says to his son: go ahead, criticize me, but strongly hints that all effective criticism will be very unwelcome" [1], p. 88.

And indeed – criticism is not always useful. Sometimes it is just "noise". The art of paragogical praxis is to make something useful out of what would otherwise just be noise. (And, note, we have hinted that for this project, effective criticism will be very welcome!)

Reference

1. Deleuze, G., and Guattari, F. (2004). *Anti-oedipus*. Continuum International Publishing Group.

Stasis

Actually, living beings are never *really* in stasis. It just sometimes feels that way. Different anti-patterns like ISOLATION or NAVEL-GAZING have described different aspects of the *experience* of feeling like one is in stasis. Typically, what is happening in such a case is that one or more dimensions of life are moving very slowly.

For instance, we were not able to get programming support to improve the first version of the Social Media Classroom, for love or money, since all developer energy was going into the next version. This isn't true stasis, but it can feel frustrating when a specific small feature is desired, but unavailable.

The solution? Don't get hung up on small things, and find the dimensions where movement *is* possible. In a sense this is analogous to eating a balanced diet. You probably shouldn't only eat grilled cheese sandwiches, even if you like them a lot. You should go for something different once in a while.

This is also related to the pattern that talks about "CARRYING CAPACITY". There is always some dimension on which you can make progress – it just might not be the same dimension you've recently over-harvested!

Stuck at the level of weak ties

Knowing how to make good use of "weak ties" is often seen as a strength.

> **Nancy Darling**: [S]trong and weak ties tend to serve different functions in our lives. When we need a big favor or social or instrumental support, we ask our friends. We call them when we need to move a washing machine. But if we need information that we don't have, the people to ask are our weak ties. They have more diverse knowledge and more diverse ties than our close friends do. We ask them when we want to know who to hire to install our washing machine. [1]

The quote suggests that there is a certain trade-off between use of weak ties and use of strong ties. The *anti-pattern* in question then is less to do with whether we are forming weak ties or strong ties, and more to do with whether we are being honest with ourselves and with each other about the nature of the ties we are forming – and their potential uses. We can be "peers" in either a weak or a strong sense. The question to ask is whether our needs match our expectations! In the peeragogy context, this has to do with how we interact.

> **One of us**: I am learning about peeragogy, but I think I'm failing to be a good peeragogue. I remember that Howard once told us that the most important thing

is that you should be responsible not only for your own learning but for your peers' learning. [...] So the question is, are we learning from others by ourselves or are we helping others to learn?

If we are "only" co-consumers of information then this seems like a classic example of a weak tie. We are part of the same "audience". On the other hand, if we are actively engaging with other people, then this is a foundation for strong ties. In this case of deep learning, our aims are neither instrumental nor informational, but "interactional". People who do not put in the time and effort will remain stuck at the level of "weak ties", and will not be able to draw on the benefits that "strong ties" offer.

Reference

1. Nancy Darling (2010). FACEBOOK AND THE STRENGTH OF WEAK TIES, Psychology Today.

CHAPTER 10

A PATTERN STORY

October, 2011. Tom's day-job involves finding patterns in market data (see KEVIN SLAVIN's TED TALK). He reads philosophy and does some other programming work in his spare time. However, he doesn't take the Occupy Wall Street protest very seriously. But one of these evenings, one of the protestors catches his attention. She's dressed rather strikingly. They talk, and he comes away thinking about something she said: "ALL OUR GRIEVANCES ARE INTERCONNECTED." What if all the solutions are interconnected too? Night time: Tom becomes increasingly obsessed with this idea. He's pulling down lots of web pages from the internet — again, looking for patterns. What would it take for OWS folks to solve the problems they worry so much about? He starts working on a tool that's geared towards learning and sharing skills, while working on real projects. At first, it's just hackers who are using the tool, but over time they adapt it for popular use. Things start to get interesting...

MULTIPLE PSK31 TRANSMISSIONS ON THE 20M DIGITAL MODES BAND AT AROUND 14.07 MHz. Based on a public domain image by User:Mysid

Part V

Convening A Group

CHAPTER 11

BUILDING YOUR CO-LEARNING GROUP

Authors: Gigi Johnson and Joe Corneli

So you've decided you want to try peer learning? Maybe you've already found a few people who will support you in this effort. Congratulations! It's time now to focus your thinking. How will you convene others to form a suitable group? How will you design a learner experience which will make your project thrive? In this chapter, we suggest a variety of questions that will help you to make your project more concrete for potential new members. There are no good or bad answers - it depends on the nature of your project and the context. Trying to answer the questions is not something you do just once. At various stages of the project, even after it's over, some or all of those questions will aquire new meanings - and probably new answers.

Fabrizio Terzi: There is a force of attraction that allows aggregation into groups based on the degree of personal interest; the ability to enhance and improve the share of each participant; and the expectation of success and potential benefit.

Group identity

Note that there are many groups that may not need to be "convened", since they already exist. There is a good story from A. T. ARIYARATNE in his COLLECTED WORKS in which he does "convene" a natural group (namely, a village) - but in any case, keep in mind at the outset that the degree of group-consciousness that is necessary for peer learning to take place is not fixed. In this section, we suppose you are just at the point of kicking off a project. What steps should you take? We suggest you take a moment to ponder the following questions first - and revisit them afterward, as a way to identify best practices for the next effort.

There will be a quiz

Those taking the initiative should ask themselves the traditional Who, What, Where, When, Why, and How. (SIMON SINEK suggests to begin with Why, and we touched on Who, above!). In doing so, preliminary assumptions for design and structure are established. However, in peer learning it is particularly important to maintain a healthy degree of openness, so that future group members can also form their answers on those questions. In particular, this suggests that the design and structure of the project (and the group) may change over time. Here, we riff on the traditional 5W's+H with six clusters of questions to help you focus your thinking about the project and amplify its positive outcomes.

"I keep six honest serving-men (They taught me all I knew)"

Expectations for participants

1. Who: Roles and flux

- What are some of the roles that people are likely to fall into (e.g. Newcomer, Wrapper, Lurker, Aggregator, etc.)?

- How likely is it that participants will stick with the project? If you expect many participants to leave, how will this effect the group and the outcome?

- Do you envision new people joining the group as time goes by? If so, what features are you designing that will support their integration into an existing flow?

- Will the project work if people dip in and out? If so, what features support that? If not, how will people stay focused?

2. What: Nature of the project

- What skills are required? What skills are you trying to build?

- What kinds of change will participants undergo? Will they be heading into new ground? Changing their minds about something? Learning about learning?

- What social objective, or "product" if any, is the project aiming to achieve?

- What's the 'hook?' Unless you are working with an existing group, or re-using an existing modality, consistent participation may not be a given.

3. When: Time management

- What do you expect the group to do, from the moment it convenes, to the end of its life-span, to create the specific outcome that will exist at the conclusion of its last meeting? (C. Gersick.) Note that what people ACTUALLY do may be different from what you envision at the outset, so you may want to revisit this question (and your answer) again as the project progresses.

- Keeping in mind that at least one period of is inertia is very likely (C. Gersick), what event(s) do you anticipate happening in the group that will bring things back together, set a new direction, or generally get things on track? More generally, what kinds of contingencies does your group face? How does it interface to the "outside world"?

- What pre-existing narratives or workflows could you copy in your group?

- How much of a time commitment do you expect from participants? Is this kind of commitment realistic for members of your group?

- What, if anything, can you do to make participation "easy" in the sense that it happens in the natural flow of life for group members?

- Does everyone need to participate equally? How might non-equal participation play out for participants down the line?

4. Where: Journey vs Destination

- What structures will support participants in their journey to the end result(s) you (or they) have envisioned? What content can you use to flesh out this structure?

- Where can the structure "flex" to accommodate unknown developments or needs as participants learn, discover, and progress?

5. Why: Tool/platform choice

- What tools are particularly suited to this group? Consider such features as learning styles and experiences, geographical diversity, the need for centralization (or decentralization), cultural expectations related to group work, sharing, and emerging leadership.

- Is there an inherent draw to this project for a given population, or are you as facilitator going to have to work at keeping people involved? How might your answer influence your choice of tools? Is the reward for completion the learning itself, or something more tangible?

- In choosing tools, how do you prioritize such values and objectives as easy entry, diverse uses, and high ceilings for sophisticated expansion?

6. How: Linearity vs Messiness

- How will your group manage feedback in a constructive way?

- Why might participants feel motivated to give feedback?

- How firm and extensive are the social contracts for this group? Do they apply to everyone equally, or do they vary with participation level?

- What do people need to know at the start? What can you work out as you go along? Who decides?

- How welcome are "meta-discussions"? What kinds of discussions are not likely to be welcome? Do you have facilities in place for "breakout groups" or other peer-to-peer interactions? (Alternatively, if the project is mostly distributed, do you have any facilities in place for coming together as a group?)

Cycles of group development

The above questions remain important thoughout the life of the project. People may come and go, particpants may propose fundamentally new approaches, people may evolve from lurkers to major content creators or vice-versa. The questions we suggest can be most effective if your group discusses them over time, as part of its workflow, using synchronous online meetings (e.g., Big Blue Button, Adobe Connect, Blackboard Collaborate), forums, Google docs, wikis, and/or email lists. Regular meetings are one way to establish a "heartbeat" for the group.

In thinking about other ways of structuring things, note that the "body" of the *Peeragogy Handbook* follows a TUCKMAN-LIKE OUTLINE (*Convening a Group* is our "forming", *Organizing a Learning Context* is our "storming and norming", *Coworking/Facilitation* is our "performing", and *Assessment* is our "adjourning"). But we agree with Gersick [1], and Engeström [2], that groups do not always follow a linear or cyclical pattern with their activities!

Nevertheless, there may be some specific stages or phases that you want *your* group to go through. Do you need some "milestones," for example? How will you know when you've achieved "success?"

In closing, it is worth reminding you that it is natural for groups to experience conflict, especially as they grow or cross other threshold points or milestones - or perhaps more likely, when they don't cross important milestones in a timely fashion (ah, so you remember those milestones from the previous section!). Nevertheless, there are some strategies can be used to make this conflict productive, rather than merely destructive (see Ozturk and Simsek [3]).

References

1. Engeström, Y. (1999). Innovative learning in work teams: Analyzing cycles of knowledge creation in practice. In Y. Engeström, R. Miettinen & R.-L-. Punamäki (Eds.), *Perspec-

tives on activity theory, (pp. 377-404). Cambridge, UK: Cambridge University Press

2. Gersick, C. (1988). Time and transition in work teams: Toward a new model of group development. *Academy of Management Journal* 31 (Oct.): 9-41.

3. Ozturk and Simsek, "OF CONFLICT IN VIRTUAL LEARNING COMMUNIITIES IN THE CONTEXT OF A DEMOCRATIC PEDAGOGY: A PARADOX OR SOPHISM?," in *Proceedings of the Networked Learning Conference, 2012, Maastricht.*

CHAPTER 12

PLAY AND LEARNING

Authors: Bryan Alexander and Anna Keune

Once more we're back to the question, "What makes learning fun?" There are deep links between play and learning. Consider, for instance, the way we learn the rules of a game through playing it. The first times we play a card game, or a physical sport, or a computer simulation we test out rule boundaries as well as our understanding. Actors and role-players learn their roles through the dynamic process of performance. The resulting learning isn't absorbed all at once, but accretes over time through an emergent process, one unfolding further through iterations. In other words, the more we play a game, the more we learn it.

In addition to the rules of play, we learn about the subject which play represents, be it a strategy game (chess, for example) or simulation of economic conflict. Good games echo good teaching practice, too, in that they structure a single player's experience to fit their regime of competence (cf. Vygotsky's zone of proximal learning, a la Gee [1]). That is to say a game challenges players at a level suited to their skill and knowledge: comfortable enough that play is possible, but so challenging as to avoid boredom, eliciting player growth. Role-playing in theater lets performers explore and test out concepts; see Boal [2]. Further, adopting a playful attitude helps individuals meet new challenges with curiosity, along with a readiness to mobilize ideas and practical knowledge. Indeed, the energy activated by play can take a person beyond an event's formal limitations, as players can assume that play can go on and on [3].

Douglas Thomas and John Seely Brown: "All systems of play are, at base, learning systems." [4]

Games have always had a major social component, and learning plays a key role in that interpersonal function. Using games to build group cohesion is an old practice, actually a triusm in team sports.

It is important to locate our peeragogical moment in a world where gaming is undergoing a renaissance. Not only has digital gaming become a large industry, but gaming has begun to infiltrate non-gaming aspects of the world, sometimes referred to as "gamification." Putting all three of these levels together, we see that we can possibly improve co-learning by adopting a playful mindset. Such a playful attitude can then mobilize any or all of the above advantages. For example,

- Two friends are learning the Russian language together. They invent a vocabulary game: one identifies an object in the world, and the other must name it in Russian. They take turns, each challenging the other, building up their common knowledge.

- A middle-aged man decides to take up hiking. The prospect is somewhat daunting, since he's a very proud person and is easily stymied by learning something from scratch. So he adopts a "trail name", a playful pseudonym. This new identity lets him set-aside his self-importance and risk making mistakes. Gradually he grows comfortable with what his new persona learns.

- We can also consider the design field as a useful kind of playful peeragogy. The person *playing the role* of the designer can select the contextual frame within which the design is performed. This frame can be seen as the *rules* governing the design, the artifact and the process. These rules, as with some games, may change over time. Therefore the possibility to adapt, to tailor one's activities to changing context is important when designing playful learning activities. (And we'll look at some ways to design peer learning experiences next!)

Of course, "game-based learning" can be part of standard pedagogy too. When peers create the game themselves, this presumably involves both game-based learning and peer learning. Classic strategy games like Go and CHESS also provide clear examples of peer learning practices: the question is partly, what skills and mindsets do our game-related practices really teach?

> **Socrates**: "No compulsory learning can remain in the soul . . . In teaching children, train them by a kind of game, and you will be able to see more clearly the natural bent of each." (quoted by Thomas Malone [5])

Exercises that can help you cultivate a playful attitude

- Use the OBLIQUE STRATEGIES card deck (Brian Eno and Peter Schmidt, 1st edition 1975, now available in its fifth edition) to spur playful creativity. Each card advises players to change their creative process, often in surprising directions.

- Take turns making and sharing videos. This online collaborative continuous video storytelling involves a group of people creating short videos, uploading them to YouTube, then making playlists of results. Similar to CLIP KINO, only online.

- Engage in theater play using Google+ Hangout. e.g. coming together with a group of people online and performing theatrical performances on a shared topic that are recorded.

References

1. Gee, J. P. (1992). *The social mind: Language, ideology, and social practice.* Series in language and ideology. New York: Bergin & Garvey.

2. Boal, A. (1979). *Theatre of the oppressed.* 3rd ed. London: Pluto Press.

3. Bereiter, C. and Scadamalia, M. (1993). *Surpassing ourselves, an inquiry into the nature and implications of expertise.* Peru, Illinois: Open Court.

4. Douglas Thomas and John Seely Brown (2011), *A New Culture of Learning: Cultivating the Imagination for a World of Constant Change.* CreateSpace.

5. Malone, T.W. (1981), Toward a Theory of Intrinsically Motivating Instruction, *Cognitive Science*, 4, pp. 333-369

CHAPTER 13

K-12 PEERAGOGY

Author: Verena Roberts

Teachers have a reputation of working in isolation, of keeping their learning to themselves and on their own islands. They are also known for generously sharing resources with one another. It is this latter trait that is becoming increasingly important as the role of the educator continues to expand. As educational technology research specialist Stephen Downes OBSERVES, the expectations on teachers have grown from "being expert in the discipline of teaching and pedagogy...[to needing to have] up-to-date and relevant knowledge and experience in it. Even a teacher of basic disciplines such as science, history or mathematics must remain grounded, as no discipline has remained stable for very long, and all disciplines require a deeper insight in order to be taught effectively." It is no longer possible for an educator to work alone to fulfil each of these roles: the solution is to work and learn in collaboration with others. This is where peer-based sharing and learning online, connected/networked learning, or peeragogy, can play an important role in helping educators.

Becoming a connected/networked learner

The following steps are set out in 'phases' in order to suggest possible experiences one may encounter when becoming connected. It is acknowledged that every learner is different and these 'phases' only serve as a guide.

Phase 1: Deciding to take the plunge To help educators begin to connect, the CONNECTED EDUCATOR'S STARTER KIT was created during Connected Educator's Month in August 2012. This article previews the main steps. The first step to becoming a 'connected educator-learner' involves making the commitment to spending the time you'll need to learn how to learn and share in an open, connected environment.

Phase 2: Lurking We start off as lurkers. A learner can be considered a true 'lurker' after reviewing the starter kit, establishing a digital presence (through a blog or a wiki) or signing up for Twitter and creating a basic profile containing a photo. In this phase, lurkers will begin to 'FOLLOW' OTHER USERS ON TWITTER and observe EDUCATIONAL TWITTER 'CHATS'. Lurkers will also begin to seek out other resources through BLOGS, FACEBOOK, EDMODO and LINKEDIN groups.

Phase 3: Entering the fray The lurker begins to develop into a connected educator-learner once he or she makes the decision to enter into a dialogue with another user. This could take the form of a personal blog post, participation on an education-related BLOG or WIKI or a an exchange with another Twitter user. Once this exchange takes place, relationships may begin to form and the work towards building a Personal Learning Network (PLN) begins.

One such site where such relationships can be built is CLASSROOM 2.0, which was founded by STEVE HARGADON. Through Classroom 2.0, Steve facilitates a number of free online learning opportunities including weekly BLACKBOARD COLLABORATE sessions, conferences, book projects and grassroots cross-country educational-transformation tours. Classroom 2.0 also offers a supportive Social Ning—a free, social learning space that provides online conferences and synchronous and recorded interviews with inspirational educators—for connected educator-learners around the world.

Phase 4: Building and shaping your PLN Just as not every person one meets becomes a friend, it is important to remember that not every exchange will lead to a co-learning peeragogy arrangement. It may be sufficient to follow another who provides useful content without expecting any reciprocation. It is dependent on each educator-learner to determine who to pay attention to and what learning purpose that individual or group will serve. It is also up to the learner-educator to demonstrate to others that he or she will actively participate.

There are a number of STRATEGIES one can use when shaping the PLN to learn. However, one of the best ways educators can attract a core of *peeragogues* is by sharing actively and demonstrating active and open learning for others.

There are a number of sites where a new educator-learner can actively and openly learn. In addition to personal blogging and wikis, other professional development opportunities include open, online courses and weekly synchronous online meetings through video, podcasts or other forms of media.

Examples include: CONNECTED LEARNING TV, TECHTALK-TUESDAYS, VOLUNTEERSNEEDED, SIMPLEK12, K12 ONLINE, CEET, and EDTECHTALK.

Alternatively, courses are offered with P2PU's School of Education or a wide variety of other opportunities collected by TEACHTHOUGHT and Educator's CPD online. Peggy George, the co-facilitator of the weekly Classroom 2.0 LIVE Sessions, created a livebinder package of free 'PD ON DEMAND' connected professional development online options for peeragogy enthusiasts.

Stage 5: Extending the digital PLN and connecting face-to-face Over time, once the connected educator-learner has established a refined PLN, these peeragogues may choose to shift their learning into physical learning spaces. Some options available for these educator-learners would include the new 'grassRoots unconferences', which include examples such as: EDUCON, ED-CAMPS, THATCAMP and CONNECTEDCA.

These (un)conferences are free or extremely low-cost and focus on learning from and with others. They are typically publicized through Twitter, Google Apps, and Facebook. Connecting face-to-face with other peeragogues can strengthen bonds to learning networks and help to promote their sustainability.

Postscript   Sylvia Tolisano, Rodd Lucier and Zoe Branigan-Pipen co-created an INFOGRAPHIC that which explores the experiences individuals may encounter in the journey to become connected learners through another related sequence of steps: *Lurker, Novice, Insider, Colleague, Collaborator, Friend,* and *Confidant.* Check it out, and also have a look at our Recommended Readings for some additional resources.

CHAPTER 14

P2P SELF-ORGANIZED LEARNING ENVIRONMENTS

Author: Jan Herder

> From this conversational piece you can engage in a journey to affect your learning space through many points of entry interacting with the physical one. We hope to inspire emerging structure and reciprocal mentoring to create a ripple effect for those willing to open the door to a new possible world.

The Guiding Strategy:

In his Peeragogical Case Study David Preston states:

> Peeragogical interaction requires refining relational and topical critique, as well as skills in other "meta" literacies, including but not limited to critical thinking, collaboration, conflict resolution, decision-making, mindfulness, patience and compassion. (from Case Study: 5PH1NX [1]).

A SELF-ORGANIZING LEARNING ENVIRONMENT, or SOLE, with a living structure accomplishes all of these outcomes, or David's "meta-literacies," simultaneously. An authentic problem and/or project based activity in a connected learning environment includes diverse learners in diverse ways by empowering all learners as peers.

This provides the authentic learning environment with which to design a SOLE. SOLEs are everywhere. How have we evolved as a species, if not through self-organizing? A conversation between strangers is self organizing, each learning about something

A VISUALIZATION OF THE FACILITATED PEER TO PEER SOLE (HTTP://GOO.GL/7STKJK)

P2P SOLE

or each other. The spaces around people conversing is also an environment, though not explicitly a learning one. While we are always self-organizing to learn or accomplish things, one place that SOLEs do not always exist are in learning institutions. In many educational institutions, our learning environments are predominately organized by the teacher, curriculum, or society. How can we nurture peer to peer learning environments to organize? How does the role of the teacher differ in a SOLE? In what ways can we unite that fundamental, passionate human characteristic of curiosity and self-organizing back into our Learning Environments?

The model that Sugata Mitra [2] is experimenting with gives us some scaffolding to create one ourselves. This is the goal of his SOLE Tool Kit (3). Sugata's kit is directed towards children between 8 and 12 years old. I was wondering if there is a way to make it more universal in its application. How can I apply it to my situation? How is a SOLE different in the context of peer to peer learning? This chapter of the Handbook uses Sugata's model as a doorway into our understanding a SOLE approach to peer to peer learning. Its three key components are: learners, context and project. I find the discussion needs to integrate what we are learning about diverse learners into a Universal Design for Learning [4] context. After all, we cannot take for granted who the peers are in the SOLE. Equally, the context, the learning environment (LE) must be as deeply considered as the learners participating. As a learning designer, I am also seeking more clues about the living structure of a well crafted SOLE.

Centers within the Center

SOLEs exist in a particular context. Take Sugata's Hole in the Wall [5] experiment. The parameters of the environment of a computer embedded in a wall in India are very specific. Sugata's act was to design a project in order to facilitate a process within that environment. The elements he introduced were a touch screen computer embedded in a wall with specific software. Sugata has abstracted this design into a Tool Kit. He speaks of

'Child Driven Learning', intrinsically motivated learning with the curiosity to learn something in particular. As a learner-centric peeragogy, SOLEs are emergent, bottom up, seeking to answer: How do we design a project (or phrase a problem) that ignites a learner's passion?

A SOLE is a facilitated learning environment (LE) that can nurture learner driven activity. For instance, in the Hole in the Wall example, the design is the context of the wall, the street, the neighborhood –and the facilitation is the touch screen monitor in the wall. They are brilliantly united. In this sense it is an intentional, self-aware learning environment. It is a strange foreign object that anyone would have to figure out how it works to take advantage of. But this is not in the classroom, or in the 'school.' It is an informal LE. Just like LEARNING A GAME [6], there is an entire ecology that surrounds you. This is very much a systemic approach. The context is facilitated explicitly (your design of the SOLE), but also implicitly in the HIDDEN CURRICULUM [7] that defines your LE. Above is the layout of the TRANSFORMED LEARNING ENVIRONMENT [8] I explored to work around the hidden curriculum of the traditional classroom. The LE has a tremendous, if not OVERWHELMING INFLUENCE, ON LEARNING [9]. The first step in connected learning is to reconnect to the environment around us. For me, the primary context of my LE is a performing arts center at a small rural liberal arts college. The Performing Arts Center is a Center within the context of the college and community. A diversity of spaces within the facility are inhabited: small and cozy, large and public, technology embedded everywhere, all focused on the project based learning that emerges producing a performance. I stay away from a formal classroom as much as possible. These spaces are Centers within the Center, 'LOOSELY CONNECTED ADAPTIVE COMPLEX SYSTEMS' [10] within themselves, just like people. I believe that the possibility of a SOLE emerging as a living structure seems to depend on the correct types of complex systems engaged in the LE.

What is the role of the internet in your design? Mitigating inequalities and accommodating diverse learners are somewhat assisted by access to the internet. But it is the immediate, JUST-

IN-TIME LEARNING [11] that makes free and open access to the world wide web so important in a SOLE. Wireless is available throughout this LE. Nooks and lounges, interconnected, but separate rooms, provide lots of places for collaboration or solitary work, for staying connected or hiding out. In a UDL vision of a facilitated peer to peer SOLE, technology is integral to the design. In the case of my LE, with the use of digital audio, multi-media, database management, robotic lighting and DICHROIC [12] colors, learners are accustomed to accessing and augmenting reality with technology: allowing learners to access their social media is part of their content creation.

Do we start our SOLE as peers? Peer to peer assumes your participants are peers–especially you, the facilitator. There needs to be enough diversity and complexity to include all learners, engendering a UNIVERSALLY DESIGNED CONTEXT [13]. What is the role of diversity in peer to peer SOLE building? How are diverse learners peers? In my LE, I discovered 70% of my learners have learning challenges. I know my LE is not unique in this regard. I have to facilitate a SOLE design that is inclusive. This is in contradistinction to commonality, yet this diversity is what we crave, for creativity and innovation, for deep learning to occur. Crafting your SOLE using multiple means of representation, expression and engagement empowers learners to be peers. A diverse learning environment, supporting diverse learning styles and diverse learners, supports a complex project based SOLE. But there are many SOLEs within the SOLE since learning is occurring on many levels with each student and within each group. We do not all get the same thing at the same time. Learning outcomes are diverse, emergent, serendipitous.

What type of project, problem or event will focus your efforts? Either a LEARNER GENERATED SYLLABUS [14] may emerge from the SOLE, or a USER GENERATED EDUCATION [15] within a specific context may answer this question. Ownership and leadership emerge when learners can apply their creativity and/or authentically assist each other in a common goal. Opportunities to design and modify even small things will draw learners into a project. The more they must rely on each other, collaborate and share their creativity, their designs and actualization–the more they work together as peers. The spaces in your LE are most likely already designed and built to accommodate the purpose of the facility in the context of the college or school. We cannot really redesign the actual space, but we can redesign many aspects. We can look for designs within it. Being able to design your own space, or project, is critical to taking ownership of your learning and experiencing the consequences. As learners mature and look for ways to be more involved, I suggest they redesign the shop, the repertory lighting plot, or the procedures of their department and/or SOLE overall. Exchanging roles as designer also stimulates peer interaction. Why not integrate design and design thinking? In my context, lighting, scene, costume and sound design are interconnected opportunities. Along with accompanying technology, every opportunity is used to nurture empathy, creativity, rationality and systems thinking. Integral to the learner generated syllabus or project design should be continuous artifact creation. A great place to start the design process and to begin to generate content is by using a virtual world.

Constant content creation can integrate assessment into your SOLE. It is the quality of the artifacts created along the way that reveals the success of your SOLE. Media that chronicles a journey through time, created by each learner, reveals the depth of participation. It is nearly impossible to cheat. The learner expresses their comprehension in the types and extent of artifact creation.

As the facilitator, I look for opportunities to introduce the unexpected, bigger questions, deeper considerations, along the way. For example, in the context of my LE, one of the events feature Tibetan Monks. They bring a counterpoint to the inflated egos and cult of personality which is prevalent in our context. The SOLE Plan is extended. It can happen over a much longer amount of time than one class or one day. The actors rehearse for weeks, as the design team designs, giving time for: research, absorption, misleads, mistakes, correction and reflection. A SOLE needs time and persistence to generate artifacts, documentation and experiences of the project and virtual worlds are an excellent way to extend time and space synchronously and asynchronously.

Sugata emphasizes the Big questions. We do not always know what they are. A focus? A goal? A product? And the event? That should be decided with the group. The learners intuit the direction that leads to deep engagement and the bigger questions. I try and leave it ambiguous, suggesting some of the things they might encounter. Facilitating the SOLE in this context, we face endless questions connected to the specific LE, to all the imaginary scenarios, Herculean tasks and questions– like building castles, programming a digital sound console, troubleshooting robotic lighting instruments, how to make the illusion of fire or, even, who killed Charlemagne? The Box Office is an example of an informal SOLE that has emerged recurrently over time. I have noticed that its vitality depends on the characters and the ebb and flow of learners entering the group or graduating. The physical space is a small, windowless and often damp room with a couple of couches and a desk with a computer squeezed in. My very own 'Hole in the Wall' experiment. The bottom of the door can remain closed, while the top is open, like a stable. Primarily the students are paid to be there, answering the phone, reserving tickets, greeting patrons and managing the Box Office and the Front of the House. In the SOLE, this subtle inversion of the institutional value proposition turns 'work study' into studying work. This is an informal LE nested within the context of the formal institution and the wider LE: a center within a center. Some semesters there are business majors working their way up the job ladder: Usher to Assistant Front of House Manager, to Assistant Box Office Manager, to Box Office Manager. Sometimes this takes 4 years, sometimes it happens in a semester or two. It is a recursive SOLE that differs as the interests and skills of the students who inhabit the space change. As the current manager puts it, the Box Office is a 'constantly evolving puzzle.'

This example of a SOLE in an informal LE is similar to the other types of SOLE's that occur within a facilitated LE. The learner's interact as reciprocal apprentices, leaning on one another to solve challenges and problems. Groups are self-selective, this type of work suits their temperament and interests, or time. This cohort is almost a clique, attracting their boyfriends and girlfriends. They begin initiatives, re-design the lobby for crowd control, redecorate and rearrange the space constantly, decide their schedules and split up responsibility. Everyone is always training everyone, because the environment turns over each semester. It is explicitly an informal LE. The workers are students. This inverts the usual state of affairs, where essentially they are being paid to learn, though they may not even be aware of it. Occasionally, the learning experience resonates deeply with them. A number of them have used the experience to leverage jobs that parallel their interests, or get them started on their careers.

Job titles, roles of responsibility, are often problematic in a SOLE. The bottom line is that as peers we are all equal and at certain times everyone is expected to do everything regardless of their roles. Titles go to people's heads. But this is part of the experience. Keep the titles moving, change it up when things get bottlenecked over personalities. Sometimes I create duplicate positions, Assistants of Assistants. and Department Heads. The Apprenticeship model is at play but in a new way in a SOLE. There are peers and there are peers. As power struggles emerge, some like-to-like grouping occurs. The role of the facilitator becomes mediator. The emergent epistemology of abundance and connected learning asks for a multitude of 'experts.' In the same way, leadership can be distributed, flowing as varying needs arise.

The experience of practicing leadership skills and encountering all the variables of working with diverse folks quickly gives feedback to us if this is a helpful role for this person. It is messy sometimes, and there are conflicts. After a few events, they learn how to manage a Box Office, dealing with patrons, emergencies, complaints and bag check. They confront the larger peer group, the student body, with authority and empathy. They are very proud of their jobs and make their own name tags with titles. A hierarchy gives them rewards that they have been trained to expect from years in school. It is another way of developing intrinsic motivation and challenges them to interact with their peers authentically.

As facilitator, I try to leave them alone as much as possible. The context has been created, the computer in the wall is on a desk. Extending the design of your SOLE contributes to its living structure. I have used Facebook as a Supplemental LMS [16] since 2007 because this is where my students are and it allows them to control the structures of groups emergently. The learners create the groups as they are relevant. The facilitator does not. Usually they invite me in! For now, Facebook aggregates the learning community that the SOLE inspires as learners become leaders, establish connections with each other and mentor newbies. This activity is integrated into artifact creation, 'comments' and documentation of their personal learning journey. Facebook becomes a precursor for their portfolios, and in some cases, it is their portfolio. Reciprocal Apprenticeships [17] occur in the dynamic of collaboration among peers. Continuity in time beyond the event horizon is accomplished by these relationships. Peers nurture one another along the shared learning journey that the SOLE provides. As facilitator and designer, you are, most of all, in a reciprocal relationship with the other learners. This is the essence of being a peer, an interaction that respects what each of us brings to the experience.

References

1. Preston, David (2014). Case Study: 5PH1NX (pp. 49–61, this volume).

2. About Sugata Mitra

3. The SOLE Toolkit

4. National Center for Universal Design for Learning, Universal Design for Learning Guidelines

5. Sugata Mitra (2010). The child-driven education, TED.

6. Game-based Learning and Intrinsic Motivation by Kristi Mead

7. Hidden Curriculum, on Wikipedia.

8. Transformed Learning Environment Analysis

9. Elmasry, Sarah Khalil (2007). Integration Patterns of Learning Technologies. IRB# 05-295-06.

10. Curious : In-Forming singular/plural design, The Theories of Christopher Alexander.

11. Overwhelmed with Blog Tips? Hack Learning with Just In Time Information

12. Dichroic Filter, on Wikipedia.

13. cast.org, UDL Guidelines

14. Active Learning Student Generated Syllabus

15. User Generated Education Blog

16. Facebook as a Supplemental LMS

17. Reciprocal Apprenticeship

CHAPTER 15

A STORY ABOUT NEW BEGINNINGS

Once he gets to the Whispering Gallery, Jorge realizes that the girl was right. This *is* the center of the universe. There are murmurs to be heard there – it seems they come from everywhere. He hears about guilds and the craftsmen who built the cathedral. He learns about how proud they were and how they formed communities of practice, educating the uninitiated, teaching each other to create. He returns to ground level. The girl is gone, but he feels happy and inspired. He can do much more then repackage social media streams; there is more going on here than Twitter as a new broadcast medium. He starts a new journey: finding a guild, a community of practice, but restyled in a 21st century fashion. It will be more open, more connected to others then the old guilds. He will still use Twitter, a social dashboard, and curating tools, but also he uses wikis, and synchronous communication. And most importantly, he starts building, together with others – in particular, together with the people formerly known as his readers. They will co-create the analysis, the search for solutions and sense-making, rather than helplessly listening to "experts", passively consuming pre-processed knowledge and information. Instead, they'll start building their own destiny, and the newsroom will be part of the platform.

Section of the Dome at St Paul's Cathedral

Part VI

Organizing a Learning Context

CHAPTER 16

INTRODUCTION TO ORGANIZING CO-LEARNING

This section about organizing Co-Learning rests on the assumption that learning always happens in a context, whether this context is a structured "course" or a (potentially) less structured "learning space". For the moment we consider the following division:

- *Organizing Co-learning Contexts*
    - Courses (= "learning linked to a timeline or syllabus")
    - Spaces (= "learning not linked to a timeline or syllabus")

This section focuses on existing learning contexts and examines in detail how they have been "organized" by their (co-)creators. At a "meta-level" of media, we can talk about this parallel structure:

- *Building Co-learning Platforms*
    - Development trajectories (e.g. "design, implement, test, repeat")
    - Platform features (e.g. forums, wikis, ownership models, etc.)

A given learning environment with have both time-like and space-like features as well as both designed-for and un-planned features. A given learning platform will encourage certain types of engagement and impose certain constraints. The question for both "teachers" and "system designers" – as well as for learners – should be: *what features best support learning?*

The answer will depend on the learning task and available resources.

For example, nearly everyone agrees that the best way to learn a foreign language is through immersion. But not everyone who wants to learn, say, French, can afford to drop everything to go live in a French-speaking country. Thus, the space-like full immersion "treatment" is frequently sacrificed for course-like treatments (either via books, CDs, videos, or ongoing participation in semi-immersive discussion groups).

System designers are also faced with scarce resources: programmer time, software licensing concerns, availability of peer support, and so forth. While the ideal platform would (magically) come with solutions pre-built, a more realistic approach recognizes that problem solving always takes time and energy. The problem solving approach and associated "learning orientation" will also depend on the task and resources at hand. The following sections will develop this issue further through some specific case studies.

Case study 1 (pilot, completed): "Paragogy" and the After Action Review.

In our analysis of our experiences as course organizers at P2PU, we (Joe Corneli and Charlie Danoff) used the US Army's technique of After Action Review (AAR). To quote from OUR PAPER [2]:

> As the name indicates, the AAR is used to review training exercises. It is important to note that while one person typically plays the role of evaluator in such a review [...] the review itself happens among peers, and examines the operations of the unit as a whole.
>
> The four steps in an AAR are:
>
> 1. Review what was supposed to happen (training plans).
> 2. Establish what happened.

3. Determine what was right or wrong with what happened.

4. Determine how the task should be done differently the next time.

The stated purpose of the AAR is to "identify strengths and shortcomings in unit planning, preparation, and execution, and guide leaders to accept responsibility for shortcomings and produce a fix."

We combined the AAR with several principles (see Discussion section below), which we felt described effective peer learning, and went through steps 1-4 for each principle to look at how well it was implemented at P2PU. This process helped generate a range of advice that could be applied at P2PU or similar institutions. By presenteding our paper at the OPEN KNOWLEDGE CONFERENCE (OKCON), we were able to meet P2PU's executive director, Philipp Schmidt, as well as other highly-involved P2PU participants; our feedback may have contributed to shaping the development trajectory for P2PU.

In addition, we developed a strong prototype for constructive engagement with peer learning that we and others could deploy again. In other words, variants on the AAR and the paragogical principles could be incorporated into future learning contexts as platform features [3] or re-used in a design/administration/moderation approach [4]. For example, we also used the AAR to help structure our writing and subsequent work on PARAGOGY.NET.

Case Study 2 (in progress): "Peeragogy".

Our particular focus in the interviews was on drawing out and emphasizing the relational dimension of students, learning experiences within their environment and, consequently, on inferring from their accounts a sense of how they perceived and indeed constituted their environment. We asked them who they learned with and from and how. A further question specifically focused on whom they regarded as their peers and how they understood their peers as a source and a site for learning." [1]

In this section, we will interview and/or survey members of the Peeragogy community with questions similar to those used by Boud and Lee [1] and then identify strengths and shortcomings as we did with the AAR above. These questions are derived from the AAR.

Questions

These were discussed, refined, and answered on an etherpad: revisions to the original set of questions are marked in italics.

1. Who have you learned with *or* from in the Peeragogy project? *What are you doing to contribute to your peers' learning?*

2. How have you been learning during the project?

3. Who are your peers in this community, and why?

4. What were your expectations of participation in this project? *And, specifically, what did you (or do you) hope to learn through participation in this project?*

5. What actually happened during your participation in this project (so far)? *Have you been making progress on your learning goals (if any; see previous question) – or learned anything unexpected, but interesting?*

6. What is right or wrong with what happened (Alternatively: how would you assess the project to date?)

7. How might the task be done differently next time? (What's "missing" here that would create a "next time", "sequel", or "continuation"?)

8. *How would you like to use the Peeragogy handbook?*

9. *Finally, how might we change the questions, above, if we wanted to apply them in your peeragogical context?*

Reflections on participants' answers

The questions were intended to help participants reflect on, and change, their practice (i.e. their style of participation). There is a tension, however, between changing midstream and learning what we might do differently next time. There is a related tension between initial structure and figuring things out as we go. Arguably, if we knew, 100%, how to do peeragogy, then we would not learn very much in writing this handbook. Difficulties and tensions would be resolved "in advance" (see earlier comments about "magical" technologies for peer production).

And yet, despite our considerable collected expertise on collaboration, learning, and teaching, there have been a variety of tensions here! Perhaps we should judge our "success" partly on how well we deal with those. Some of the tensions highlighted in the answers are as follows:

1. *Slow formation of "peer" relationships.* There is a certain irony here: we are studying "peeragogy" and yet many respondents did not feel they were really getting to know one another "as peers", at least not yet. Those who did have a "team" or who knew one another from previous experiences, felt more peer-like in those relationships. Several remarked that they learned less from other individual participants and more from "the collective" or "from everyone". At the same time, some respondents had ambiguous feelings about naming individuals in the first question: "I felt like I was going to leave people out and that that means they would get a bad grade - ha!" One criterion for being a peer was to have built something together, so by this criterion, it stands to reason that we would only slowly become peers through this project.

2. *"Co-learning", "co-teaching", "co-producing"?* One respondent wrote: "I am learning about peeragogy, but I think I'm failing [to be] a good peeragog. I remember that Howard [once] told us that the most important thing is that you should be responsible not only for your own learning but

for your peers' learning. [...] So the question is, are we learning from others by ourselves or are we [...] helping others to learn?" Another wrote: "To my surprise I realized I could contribute organizationally with reviews, etc. And that I could provide some content around PLNs and group process. Trying to be a catalyst to a sense of forward movement and esprit de corps."

3. *Weak structure at the outset, versus a more "flexible" approach.* One respondent wrote: "I definitely think I do better when presented with a framework or scaffold to use for participation or content development. [...] (But perhaps it is just that I'm used to the old way of doing things)." Yet, the same person wrote: "I am interested in [the] applicability [of pæragogy] to new models for entrepreneurship enabling less structured aggregation of participants in new undertakings, freed of the requirement or need for an entrepreneurial visionary/source/point person/proprietor." There is a sense that some confusion, particularly at the beginning, may be typical for peeragogy. With hindsight, one proposed "solution" would be to "have had a small group of people as a cadre that had met and brainstormed before the first live session [...] tasked [with] roles [and] on the same page".

4. *Technological concerns.* There were quite a variety, perhaps mainly to do with the question: how might a (different) platform handle the tension between "conversations" and "content production"? For example, will Wordpress help us "bring in" new contributors, or would it be better to use an open wiki? Another respondent noted the utility for many readers of a take-away PDF version. The site (peeragogy.org) should be "[a] place for people to share, comment, mentor and co-learn together in an ongoing fashion."

5. *Sample size.* Note that answers are still trickling in. How should we interpret the response rate? Perhaps what matters is that we are getting "enough" responses to make an

analysis. One respondent proposed asking questions in a more ongoing fashion, e.g., asking people who are leaving: "What made you want to quit the project?"

Discussion

> **Lisewski and Joyce**: In recent years, the tools, knowledge base and discourse of the learning technology profession has been bolstered by the appearance of conceptual paradigms such as the 'five stage e-moderating model' and the new mantra of 'communities of practice'. This paper will argue that, although these frameworks are useful in informing and guiding learning technology practice, there are inherent dangers in them becoming too dominant a discourse.

The following table helps to emphasize something we saw in the pattern catalog: in practice, what we really have is a patchwork collection of tricks or heuristics. The paragogy principles are themselves a non-linear interface that we can plug into and adapt where appropriate. Instead of a grand narrative, we see a growing collection of case studies and descriptive patterns. As we share our experiences and make needed adaptations, our techniques for doing peer learning and peer production become more robust. Based on the experiences described above, here are a few things people may want to try out in future projects:

- "Icebreaking" techniques or a "buddy system"; continual refactoring into teams.

- Maintain a process diagram that can be used to "triage" new ideas and effort.

- Prefer the "good" to the "best", but make improvements at the platform level as needed.

- Gathering some information from everyone who joins, and, if possible, everyone who leaves.

Paragogical Principles...	Reflections on practice and experience suggest...
1. *Changing context as a decentered center.* [We interact by changing the space.]	It seems we begin with weak ties, and then experience a slow formation of "peer" relationships, as we form and re-form our social context, and come to better understand our goals.
2. *Meta-learning as a font of knowledge.* [We interact by changing what we know about ourselves.]	We learn a lot about ourselves by interacting with others. But participants struggle to find the right way to engage: "co-learning", "co-teaching", or "co-producing"? Moreover, "People come–they stay for a while, they flourish, they build–and they go."
3. *Peers provide feedback that would not be there otherwise.* [We interact by changing our perspective on things.]	We begin with a weak structure at the outset but this may afford a more "flexible" approach as time goes on (see also this handbook section which offers advice on designing activities that help create a "flexible structure").
4. *Paragogy is distributed and nonlinear.* [We interact by changing the way things connect.]	There are a number of technological concerns, which in a large part have to do with tensions between "content production" and "conversation", and to a lesser extent critique the platforms we're using.
5. *Realize the dream if you can, then wake up!* [We interact by changing our objectives.]	Even with a small group, we can extract meaningful ideas about peer learning and form a strong collective effort, which moves things forward for those involved: this means work. We would not get the same results through "pure contemplation".

References

1. Boud, D. and Lee, A. (2005). 'PEER LEARNING' AS PEDAGOGIC DISCOURSE FOR RESEARCH EDUCATION. *Studies in Higher Education*, 30(5):501–516.

2. Joseph Corneli and Charles Jeffrey Danoff, PARAGOGY, in Sebastian Hellmann, Philipp Frischmuth, Sören Auer, and Daniel Dietrich (eds.), *Proceedings of the 6th Open Knowledge Conference, Berlin, Germany, June 30 & July 1, 2011,*

3. Joseph Corneli and Alexander Mikroyannidis (2011). PERSONALISED AND PEER-SUPPORTED LEARNING: THE PEER-TO-PEER LEARNING ENVIRONMENT (P2PLE), *Digital Education Review*, 20.

4. Joseph Corneli, PARAGOGICAL PRAXIS, *E-Learning and Digital Media* (ISSN 2042-7530), Volume 9, Number 3, 2012

5. Lisewski, B., and P. Joyce (2003). Examining the Five Stage e-Moderating Model: Designed and Emergent Practice in the Learning Technology Profession, *Association for Learning Technology Journal*, 11, 55-66.

CHAPTER 17

ADDING STRUCTURE WITH ACTIVITIES

In the introduction to "Organizing a Learning Context", we remarked that a "learning space" is *only potentially* less structured than a "course". For example, a library tends to be highly structured, with quiet rooms for reading, protocols for checking out books, a cataloging and shelving system that allows people to find what they are looking for, as well as rules that deter vandalism and theft. (Digital libraries don't need to play by all the same rules, but are still structured.)

But more structure does not always lead to better learning. In a 2010 Forbes article titled, "The Classroom in 2020," George Kembel describes a future in which "Tidy lectures will be supplanted by messy real-world challenges." The Stanford School of Design, (or "d.school" – which Kemble co-founded and currently directs) is already well-known for its open collaborative spaces, abundant supply of post-it notes and markers, and improvisational brainstorm activities – almost the opposite of traditional lecture-based learning.

One "unexpected benefit" of dealing with real-world challenges is that we can change our approach as we go. This is how it works in peer learning: peers can decide on different structures not just once (say, at the beginning of a course), but throughout the duration of their time together. This way, they are never "stuck" with existing structures, whether they be messy or clean. At least... that's the ideal.

In practice, "bottlenecks" frequently arise. For example, in a digital library context, there may be bottlenecks having to do with software development, organizational resources, community good will, or access to funding – and probably all of the above. In a didactic context, it may be as simple as one person knowing something that others do not.

While we can't eliminate scarcity in one stroke, we can design activities for peer learning that are "scarcity aware" and that help us move in the direction of adaptive learning structures.

Planning Peer Learning Activities

We begin with two simple questions:

- How do we select an appropriate learning activity?

- How do we go about creating a learning activity if we don't find an existing one?

"Planning a learning activity" should mean planning an *effective* learning activity, and in particular that means something that people can and will engage with. In short, an appropriate learning activity may be one that you already do! At the very least, current activities can provide a "seed" for even more effective ones.

But when entering unfamiliar territory, it can be difficult to know where to begin. And remember the bottlenecks mentioned above? When you run into difficulty, ask yourself: why is this hard? You might try adapting ZED SHAW'S TASK-MANAGEMENT TRICK, and make a list of limiting factors, obstacles, etc., then cross off those which you can find a strategy to deal with (add an annotation as to why). For example, you might decide to overcome your lack of knowledge in some area by hiring a tutor or expert consultant, or by putting in the hours learning things the hard way (Zed would particularly approve of this choice). If you can't find a strategy to deal with some issue, presumably you can table it, at least for a while.

Strategic thinking like this works well for one person. What about when you're planning activities for someone else? Here you have to be careful: remember, this is peer learning, not traditional "teaching" or "curriculum design". The first rule of thumb for *peer learning* is: don't plan activities for others unless you plan to to take part as a fully engaged participant. Otherwise, in you might be more interested in the literature on *collaborative learning*, which has often been deployed to good effect within a standard pedagogical context (see e.g. Bruffee [1]). In a peer learning

Adding structure

setting, everyone will have something to say about "what do you need to do" and "why is it hard," and everyone is likely to be interested in everyone else's answer as well as their own.

For example, in a mathematics learning context, you would be likely to find people...

- solving textbook-style problems;

- finding and sharing new research problems;

- asking questions when something seems too difficult;

- fixing expository material to respond to critique;

- offering critique and review of proposed solutions;

- offering constructive feedback to questions (e.g. hints);

- organizing material into structured collections;

- working on applications to real-world problems;

- doing "meta" research activities that analyse "what works" for any and all of the above.

Each one of those activities may be "hard" for one reason or another. As a system the different activities tend to depend on one another. If you have people working in a "student role" but no one who can take on a "TA role", things will be more difficult for the students. As a (co-)organizer, part of *your* job is to try to make sure all of the relevant roles are covered by someone (who may in the end wear many hats). You can further decompose each role into specific concrete activities. They might be accompanied by instructions that say: "*How to write a good critique*" or "*How to write a proof*". They might come in the form of accessible exercises (where "accessible" depends on the person). Depending on the features of the learning context, you may be able to support the written instructions or exercises with live/in-person feedback (e.g. meta-critique to coach and guide novice critics, a demonstration, etc.).

One scenario: building activities for the Peeragogy Handbook

Adding a bunch of activities to the handbook won't solve all of our usability issues, but more activities would help. We can think about each article or section from this perspective:

1. When looking at this piece of text, what type of knowledge are we (and the reader) trying to gain? Technical skills, or abstract skills? What's the point?

2. What's difficult here? What might be difficult for someone else?

3. What learning activity recipes or models might be appropriate? (See e.g. [2], [3].)

4. What customizations do we need for this particular application?

As a quick example: designing a learning activity for the current page

1. *We want to be able to come up with effective learning activities, for instance, to accompany a "how to" article for peer learners. These activities will extend from from the written word to the world of action.*

2. *It might be difficult for some of us to "unplug" from all the reading and writing that we're habituated to doing. But peer learning isn't just about the exchange of text: there are lots and lots of ways to learn.*

3. *Like Tom in "A pattern story", it could be useful to apply an existing set of skills to a new problem.*

4. *The proposed handbook activity is to simply step away from the handbook for a while. Look for some examples of peer learning in everyday life. When you've gained an insight about peer from your own experience, come back and create a related activity to accompany another handbook page!*

References

1. Bruffee, Kenneth A. (1984). "Collaborative learning and the conversation of mankind." *College English* 46.7, 635-652

2. KS Toolkit

3. Designing Effective and Innovative Sources (particularly the section on "Teaching Strategies for Actively Engaging Students in the Classroom")

CHAPTER 18

THE STUDENT AUTHORED SYLLABUS

Author: Suz Burroughs

In either formal learning, informal learning or models which transition between the two, there are many opportunities for learners to co-create the syllabus and/or outline their own course of action. The *sage on the stage* of formal instruction must become at the most *a guide on the side* who acts as a coach appearing only when needed rather than as a lecturer who determines the content that the learners need to master. In the following inspirational but certainly not prescriptive examples, we will focus on co-learning methods drawn from a Social Constructivist perspective, which fits nicely here.

We offer a few examples below to show a range of learner centered approaches. They all are based on co-learners hosting each other for one of a number of digestible topics in the larger subject area or domain that the group formed in order to explore. This can take place across a number of media and timelines.

The following methods will result in each co-learner gaining deep knowledge in a specific topic and moderate knowledge across several topics. The unique joy of this approach is that no two cohorts will ever be the same. The content will always be fresh, relevant, and changing. A group can even reconvene with slightly or dramatically different topics over and over using the same underlying process.

The appropriateness of the learner-created syllabus technique depends on two factors: 1) the involvement of experts in the group and 2) the level of proficiency of the group. In general, novices who may or may not have a deep interest in the subject matter benefit from more structure and experts who point to key concepts and texts. An example of this is the university survey course for first or second year students who, we assume, need more guidance as they enter the subject matter. Graduate seminars are generally much more fluid, open dialogues between motivated experts require little structure or guidance.

We also need effective methods for groups which contain novices, experts, and everyone in between. In groups with a wide range of expertise, it is important that each co-learner chooses to focus their deep inquiry on a topic that they are less familiar with. This will *even out* the expertise level across the cohort as well as ensure that a co-learner is neither bored nor dominating the dialogue.

3 example designs to structure the learning

Weekly topics structure

One way to structure the course is to have each co-learner host a topic each week. Perhaps multiple students host their topics in the same week. This progression provides a rotation of presentations and activities to support the entire group in engaging with the topics and challenges to the thinking of the presenters in a constructive and respectful manner.

> *Pro:* co-learners have discrete timelines and manageable chunks of responsibility.
>
> *Con:* the format may become disjointed, and the depth of inquiry will likely be somewhat shallow.

Milestone based structure

In this structure, each co-learner host their topics in parallel with similar activities and milestones that the whole group moves through together. Milestones can be set for a certain date, or the group can *unlock* their next milestone whenever all participants have completed the previous milestone. This second milestone timeline can be great for informal groups where participation levels may vary from week to week due to external factors, and the sense of responsibility and game-like levels can be motivating for many co-learners.

Each co-learner may start with a post of less than 500 words introducing the topic on a superficial level. When everyone has done this, the group might move on to posting questions to the post authors. Then, there may be a summary post of the activity so far with critical recommendations or insights.

> *Pro:* co- learners have more time to digest a topic, formulate a complex schema, and generate deeper questions.

> *Con:* it will be a few weeks before the topic level schema can form into a broader understanding of the subject matter or domain (seeing the big picture takes longer).

Relay learning structure.

This is similar to the milestone structure. However, co-learners rotate topics. If one learner posts an introductory write-up on a topic the first cycle, they may be researching questions on another topic in the next cycle, posting a summary in a third, and then posting a summary on their original topic in the fourth.

> *Pro:* co-learners can experience responsibility for several topics.

> *Con:* co-learners may receive a topic that is poorly researched or otherwise neglected.

Content

A vast number of topics

Within a subject of mutual interest to a group, there are a considerable number of topics or questions. What is important is that each co-learner can take responsibility for a reasonably narrow area given the duration of the course or the timeline of the group. Areas that are too broad will result in a very superficial understanding, and areas that are too narrow will result in a dull experience. For example, in marine biology, topics such as "the inter-tidal zone" may be too broad for a course cycle of a few weeks. Narrowing to one species may be too specific for a course over a few months.

Learner generated topics

Most cohorts will have some knowledge of the shared area of interest or an adjacent area. It is a good idea to respect the knowledge and experience that each member of the group brings to the table. A facilitator or coordinator may generate a list of potential topic areas, setting an example of the scale of a topic. We suggest that the participants in the group are also polled for additions to the list. In large courses, sending out a Google Form via email can be an effective way to get a quick list with a high response rate.

Expert informed topics

If there is no expert facilitator in the group, we suggest that the cohort begin their journey with a few interviews of experts to uncover what the main buzz words and areas of focus might be. One way to locate this type of expert help is through contacting authors in the subject matter on social networks, reviewing their posts for relevance, and reaching out with the request.

We recommend two people interview the expert over video chat, for example in a Hangout. One person conducts the interview, and one person takes notes and watches the time. We strongly suggest that the interview be outlined ahead of time:

> *Warm up*: Who are you, what are your goals, and why do you think this interview will help?
>
> *Foundational questions*: Ask a few questions that might elicit short answers to build rapport and get your interviewee talking.
>
> *Inquiry*: What people say and what they do can often be very different. Ask about topics required for mas-

tery of the subject matter (e.g. What are the areas someone would need to know about to be considered proficient in this subject?). Also, ask QUESTIONS THAT REQUIRE STORYTELLING. Avoid SUPERLATIVE or CLOSE-ENDED QUESTIONS.

Wrap up: Thank the interviewee for his or her time, and be sure to follow up by sharing both what you learned and what you accomplished because he or she helped you.

Shared goals and group norms

Choosing useful outputs

Getting together for the sake of sharing what you know in an informal way can be fairly straightforward and somewhat useful. Most groups find that a common purpose and output that are explicitly defined and documented help to engage, motivate, and drive the group. For the examples above, the group may decide to create a blog with posts on the various topics or create a wiki where they can share their insights. Other outputs can include community service projects, business proposals, recommendations to senior management or administration, new products, and more. The key is to go beyond sharing for sharing sake and move toward an output that will be of use beyond the co-learning group. This activity is best described in CONNECTIVIST theory as the special case of networked learning where we find evidence of learning in collective action and/or behavioral change in groups rather than a psychological or neurological process in individuals.

Group cohesion (a.k.a. the rules of the road)

One challenge of this kind of collaboration is that each group will need to decide on norms, acceptable practices and behaviors. Culturally diverse groups in particular may run into communication or other issues unless there is a way to create shared expectations and communicate preferences.

One way to do this is with a team charter. This is a living document where the initial rules of engagement can live for reference. The group may add or edit this document over time based on experience, and that is a welcome thing! This documentation is a huge asset for new members joining the group who want to contribute quickly and effectively. Any co-editing word processing program will work, but we strongly recommend something that can be edited simultaneously and that lives in the cloud. (Google Docs is convenient because you can also embed your Charter into another site.)

Try starting with the following three sections, and allow some time for the group to co-edit and negotiate the document between icebreakers and kicking off the official learning process.

> *Mission:* Why are you forming the group? What do you want to accomplish together?
>
> *Norms:* Use NETIQUETTE? No FLAMING? Post your vacation days to a SHARED CALENDAR? Other cultural norms?
>
> *Members:* It is useful to include a photo and a link to a public profile such as Twitter, Google+ or Facebook.

Assessments and feedback loops

Co-authored assessment rubrics

Tests. Quizzes. Exams. How can the co-learning group assess their performance?

These types of courses benefit from an approach similar to coaching. Set goals as individuals and a group in the beginning, define what success looks like, outline steps that are needed to achieve the goal, check in on the goal progress periodically, and assess the results at the end of the course against the goal criteria. Goals may include domain expertise, a business outcome, a paper demonstrating mastery, a co-created resource, or even the quality of collaboration and adherence to shared group norms.

Learner created assessments

Another effective way to create an assessment is to decide on an individual or group output and create a peer assessment rubric based on the goals of the individual or group.

One way to create a rubric is to spend some time defining the qualities you want your output to have based on positive examples. Perhaps a group wants to create a blog. Each person on the team may identify the qualities of a great blog post based on examples that they admire. They can use that example to create a criteria for assessment of co-learner authored blog posts. We recommend that the criteria have a 0 to 5 point scale with 0 being non-existent and 5 being superb. Writing a few indicators in the 1, 3, and 5 columns helps to calibrate reviewers.

Create a SHARED DOCUMENT, perhaps starting with a list of criteria. Collapse similar criteria into one item, and create the indicators or definitions of 1, 3, and 5 point performance. Agree on the rubric, and decide on how the co-learners will be assigned assessment duties. WIll everyone review at least two others? Will each co-learner product need at least 3 reviewers before it goes live? Will you use a SPREADSHEET or a FORM to collect the assessments?

In a university setting, the instructor of record may wish to approve a peer assessment rubric, and it is sometimes a good idea to have a few outside experts give feedback on criteria that the group may have missed.

Outside assessments

It is possible that an instructor of record or similar authority will create the assessment for performance. In these cases, it is crucial that the co-learners have access to the grading rubric ahead of time so that they can ensure their activities and timeline will meet any requirements. In this case, it may be possible to require that the co-learners self-organize entirely, or there may be intermediary assignments such as the charter, project plan or literary review.

Cyclical use of these models

So much more to learn

As mentioned above, the joy of this type of learning is that no two groups will ever do it the same. Their process, goals, and outcomes can all be unique. As designers and facilitators of this type of learning environment, we can say it is a wild ride! Each class is exciting, refreshing, and on trend. The co-learners become our teachers.

If a group generates more topics than it is possible to cover at one time given the number of group members or if a group has plans to continue indefinitely, it is always possible to set up a system where potential topics are collected at all times. These unexplored topics can be harvested for use in another learning cycle, continuing until the group achieves comprehensive mastery.

Risks

This format is not without its own unique pitfalls: some challenges are learner disorientation or frustration in a new learning structure with ambiguous expectations and uneven participation. Some groups simply never gel, and we do not know why they have failed to achieve the cohesion required to move forward. Other groups are the exact opposite. Here are a few risks to consider if you would like to try the methods suggested here and how to mitigate them.

> *Uneven expertise:* Ask co-learners to be responsible for topics that are new to them.
>
> *Uneven participation and cohesion:* Ask co-learners what they want to do to motivate the group rather than imposing your own ideas.

Experts/facilitators that kill the conversation: In the charter or other documentation, explicitly state that the purpose of the discussion is to further the conversation, and encourage experts to allow others to explore their own thinking by asking probing (not leading) questions.

Ambiguous goals: Encourage the group to document their mission and what they will do as a team. This can change over time, but it is best to start out with a clear purpose.

Conclusion

Make mistakes. Correct course. Invite new perspectives. Create a structure that everyone can work with. Change it when it breaks. Most of all, have fun!

CHAPTER 19

CONNECTIVISM IN PRACTICE — HOW TO ORGANIZE A CMOOC

Author: Roland Legrand

Massive Open Online Courses (MOOCs) are online learning events that can take place synchronously and asynchronously for months. Participants assemble to hear, see, and participate in backchannel communication during live lectures. They read the same texts at the same time, according to a calendar. Learning takes place through self-organized networks of participants, and is almost completely decentralized: individuals and groups create blogs or wikis around their own interpretations of the texts and lectures, and comment on each other's work; each individual and group publicises their RSS feed, which are automatically aggregated by a special (freely available) tool, gRSShopper. Every day, an email goes out to all participants, aggregating activity streams from all the blogs and wikis that engage that week's material. MOOCs are a practical application of a learning theory known as "connectivism" that situates learning in the networks of connections made between individuals and between texts.

Not all MOOCs are Connectivist MOOCs (or *cMOOCs*). Platforms such as COURSERA, EDX and UDACITY offering MOOCs which follow a more traditional, centralized approach (these are sometimes called *xMOOCs*). In this type of MOOC, a professor is taking the lead and the learning-experience is organized top-down. However, some xMOOCs seem to adopt a more blended approach. For instance, the course E-LEARNING AND DIGITAL CULTURES makes use of online spaces beyond the Coursera environment, and the course organizers want some aspects of participation in this course to involve the wider social web.

In this chapter we'll focus on cMOOCs. One might wonder why a course would want to be 'massive' and what '*massive*' means. cMOOC-pioneer Stephen Downes explains that his focus is on the development of a *network structure*, as opposed to a *group structure*, to manage the course. In a network structure there isn't any central focus, for example, a central discussion. That's also the reason why he considers the figure of 150 active participants – *Dunbar's Number* – to be the lower cut-off in order to talk about 'massive':

> **Stephen Downes**: Why Dunbar's number? The reason is that it represents the maximum (theoretical) number of people a person can reasonably interact with. How many blogs can a person read, follow and respond to? Maybe around 150, if Dunbar is correct. Which means that if we have 170 blogs, then the blogs don't constitute a 'core' - people begin to be selective about which blogs they're reading, and different (and interacting) subcommunities can form.

A learning theory for the digital age

Traditionally, scholars distinguish between three main CATEGORIES OF LEARNING THEORIES: *behaviorism, cognitivism* and *constructivism*. Stephen Downes and others would add a fourth one: CONNECTIVISM, but this is DISPUTED. The central application of connectivism to date is as a theory of what happens in Massive Open Online Courses.

The connectivist theory describes learning as a process of creating connections and developing networks. It is based on the premise that knowledge exists out in the world, rather than inside an individual's mind. Connectivism sees the network as a central metaphor for learning, with a node in the network being a concept (data, feelings, images, etc.) that can be meaningfully related to other nodes. Not all connections are of equal strength in this metaphor; in fact, many connections may be quite weak.

On a practical level, this approach recommends that learning should focus on where to find information (streams), and how to evaluate and mash up those streams, rather than trying to enter lots of (perishable) information into one's skull. Knowing the pipes is more important than knowing what exactly each pipe contains at a given moment. This is the theory. The practice takes place in Connectivist MOOCs (cMOOCs), like CHANGE11. Here, people are free to participate at will. Each week a subject is discussed during synchronous sessions, which are recorded and uploaded for reference on the Change11 website. The site also includes an archive of daily newsletters and RSS-feeds of blog posts and tweets from participants.

cMOOCs tend to be learner-centered. People are encouraged to pursue their own interests and link up with others who might help them. But the distributed and free nature of the projects also leads to complaints; participants often find it confusing when they attempt to follow up on all the discussions (the facilitators say one should not try to follow up on *all* the content).

> **Stephen Downes**: This implies a pedagogy that (a) seeks to describe 'successful' networks (as identified by their properties, which I have characterized as diversity, autonomy, openness, and connectivity); and (b) seeks to describe the practices that lead to such networks, both in the individual and in society (which I have characterized as modeling and demonstration (on the part of a teacher) and practice and reflection (on the part of a learner).

Anatomy of a cMOOC

One example of a MOOC that claims to embody the connectivist theory is CHANGE.MOOC.CA. The "HOW IT WORKS" section of the site explains what connectivism means in practice. The MOOC organizers developed a number of ways to combine the distributed nature of the discussions with the need for a constantly updated overview and for a federated structure. So, if your team wants to organize an open online course, these are five points to take into consideration:

There is no body of content the participants have to memorize, but the learning results from activities they undertake. The activities are different for each person. A course schedule with suggested reading, assignments for synchronous or asynchronous sessions is provided (e.g. using Google Docs spreadsheets internally, Google Calendar externally; one could also use a wiki), but participants are free to pick and choose what they work on. Normally there is a topic, activities, reading resources and often a guest speaker for each week. One should even reflect upon the question whether a start- and end date are actually needed. It is crucial to explain the particular philosophy of this kind of MOOC, and this right from the outset, because chances are learners will come with expectations informed by their more traditional learning experiences.

1. It is important to discuss the "internal" aspects, such as self-motivation: what do the participants want to achieve, what is their larger goal? And what are their intentions when they select certain activities (rather than other possibilities)? Everyone has her own intended outcome. Suggest that participants meditate on all this and jot down their objectives. And how can they avoid becoming stressed out and getting depressed because they feel they cannot "keep up with all this?" The facilitators should have a good look at these motivations, even if it's impossible to assist every participant individually (for large-scale MOOCs).

2. Ideally, participants should prepare for this course by acquiring the necessary digital skills. Which skills are "necessary" can be decided by the group itself in advance. It's all about selecting, choosing, remixing - also called "curating". There are lots of tools which you can use for this: blogs, social bookmarks, wikis, mindmaps, forums, social dashboards, networks such as Twitter with their possibilities such as hashtags and lists. Maybe these tools are self-evident for some, but not necessarily for all the participants.

3. The course is not located in one place but is distributed across the web: on various blogs and blogging platforms, on various groups and online networks, on photo- and video-sharing platforms, on mindmaps and other visualization platforms, on various tools for synchronous sessions. This wide variety is in itself an important learning element.

4. There are weekly synchronous sessions (using Blackboard collaborate, or similar group chatting tool). During these sessions, experts and participants give presentations and enter into discussions. Groups of participants also have synchronous meetings at other venues (such as Second Life). Try to plan this well in advance!

5. Many participants highly appreciate efforts to give an overview of the proceedings. Specifically, the DAILY NEWSLETTER is a kind of hub, a community newspaper. In that Daily there is also a list of the blog posts mentioning the course-specific tag (e.g. "Change11"), also the tweets with hashtag #change11 are listed in the Daily. Of course, the MOOC has a SITE where sessions, newsletters and other resources are archived and discussion threads can be read.

From the very beginning of the course, it's necessary to explain the importance of tagging the various contributions, to suggest a hashtag.

For harvesting all this distributed content, Stephen Downes advocates the use of GRSSHOPPER, which is a personal web environment that combines resource aggregation, a personal dataspace, and personal publishing (Downes developed it and would like to build a hosted version - eventually financed via Kickstarter). The gRSShopper can be found on a registration page, which is useful primarily for sending the newsletter. It allows you to organize your online content any way you want, to import content - your own or others' - from remote sites, to remix and repurpose it, and to distribute it as RSS, web pages, JSON data, or RSS feeds.

Stephen Downes: For example, the gRSShopper harvester will harvest a link from a given feed. A person, if he or she has admin privileges, can transform this link into a post, adding his or her own comments. The post will contain information about the original link's author and journal. Content in gRSShopper is created and manipulated through the use of system code that allows administrators to harvest, map, and display data, as well as to link to and create their own content. gRSShopper is also intended to act as a fully-fledged publishing tool.

Alternatives for registrations: Google Groups for instance. But specific rules about privacy should be dealt with: what will be the status of the contributions? In this MOOC the status is public and open by default, for Downes this is an important element of the course.

Technologies

Some MOOCs use Moodle, but Downes dislikes the centralization aspect and it's not as open as it could be, saying "people feel better writing in their own space." Other possibilities: Google Groups, Wordpress, Diigo, Twitter, Facebook page, Second Life; but each course uses different mixtures of the many tools out there. People choose their environment - whether it is WoW or Minecraft. Students use Blogger, WordPress, Tumblr, Posterous as blogging tools.

RSS harvesting is a key element

Give participants a means to contribute their blogfeed. In "ADD A NEW FEED," Downes explains how to get this structure and additional explanations (via videos) in order to contribute their blog feed. The administrator in this case uses gRSShopper to process the content and put it in a database, process it and send it to other people. Alternatively one can use Google Reader (the list of feeds is available as an OPML file - which can be imported to other platforms). There is also a plug-in for Wordpress that lets you use a Google Doc spreadsheet for the feeds, then Wordpress for the aggregation). Many other content management systems have RSS harvesting features.

Each individual could run her own aggregator, but Downes offers it as a service. But aggregators are needed, whether individual, centralized or both.

Specialized harvesting

Using Twitter, Diigo, Delicious, Google Groups, If This Then That (IFTTT) and FEED43 (take ordinary web page and turn it into an RSS feed).

Synchronous environments

Synchronous platforms include Blackboard Collaborate (used now for Change11); Adobe Connect; Big Blue Button; WizIQ; Fuze; WebX; webcasting; web radio; videoconferencing with Skype or Google Hangout in conjunction with Livestream or ustream.tv. Or take the Skype/Hangout audiostream and broadcast is as webradio. Set up and test ahead of time, but don't hesitate to experiment. Note also, there is a more extensive discussion of real-time tools in another section of the handbook.

Newsletter or Feeds

Feeds are very important (see earlier remarks about the Daily newsletter). You can use Twitter or a Facebook page, Downes uses email, also creates an RSS version through gRSShopper and sends it through Ifttt.com back to Facebook and Twitter. For the rest of us there is Wordpress, which you can use to CREATE AN EMAIL NEWS LETTER. Downs also suggests this handy guide on HOW TO DESIGN AND BUILD AN EMAIL NEWSLETTER WITHOUT LOOSING YOUR MIND!

Consider using a content management system and databases to put out specialized pages and the newsletter in an elegant way, but it requires a learning curve. Otherwise, use blogs / wikis.

The Use of Comments

Participants are strongly encouraged to comment on each others' blogs and to launch discussion threads. By doing so they practice a fundamental social media skill - developing networks by commenting on various places and engaging in conversations. It is important to have activities and get people to be involved rather than sit back. For an in-depth presentation, have a look at FACILITATING A MASSIVE OPEN ONLINE COURSE by Stephen Downes, in which he focuses on research and survey issues, preparing events, and other essentials.

Resources

- Change MOOC: HOW THIS COURSE WORKS
- WHAT IS A MOOC (video)
- SUCCESS IN A MOOC (video)
- KNOWLEDGE IN A MOOC (video)
- INTRODUCTION AND INVITATION (video)

CHAPTER 20

CASE STUDY: COLLABORATIVE EXPLORATIONS

Part I (by Peter Taylor).

Collaborative Exploration invites participants to shape their own directions of inquiry and develop their skills as investigators and teachers (in the broadest sense of the word). The basic mode of a Collaborative Exploration centers on interactions over a delimited period of time in small groups. Engagement takes place either online, for instance via Google+, or face-to-face. The aim is to create an experience of re-engagement with oneself as an avid learner and inquirer. This section combines practical information about how to run Collaborative Explorations as well as ideas and questions about how to make sense of what happens in them. A companion entry conveys one participant's experience with several Collaborative Explorations (hereafter, "CE").

Overview and contrast to cMOOCs

The tangible goal of any CE is to develop contributions to the topic defined by the "case", which is written by the host or originator of the CE in advance, and which is intended to be broad and thought-provoking (some examples are given below). We aim for a parallel experiential goal, which is that we hope participants will be impressed at how much can be learned with a small commitment of time using this structure. The standard model for an online CE is to have four sessions spaced one week apart, in which the same small group interacts in real time via the internet, for an hour per session. Participants are asked to spend at least 90 minutes between sessions on self-directed inquiry into the case, and to share their inquiries-in-progress with their small group and a wider community. Reflection typically involves shifts in participants' definition of what they want to find out and how. Any participants wondering how to define a meaningful and useful line of inquiry are encouraged to review the scenario for the CE, any associated materials, posts from other participants, and think about what they would like to learn more about or dig deeper into. Everyone is left, in the end, to judge for themselves whether what interests them is meaningful and useful. During the live sessions, participants can expect to do a lot of listening, starting off in the first session with autobiographical stories that make it easier to trust and take risks with whoever has joined that CE, and a lot of writing to gather their thoughts, sometimes privately, sometimes shared. There is no assumption that participants will pursue the case beyond the limited duration of the CE. This said, the tools and processes that the CE employs for purposes of inquiry, dialogue, reflection, and collaboration are designed to be readily learned by participants, and to translate well into other settings – for instance, where they can be used to support the inquiries of others. In short, online CEs are moderate-sized open online collaborative learning. It remains to be seen whether the CE "movement" will attract enough participants to scale up to multiple learning communities around any given scenario, each hosted by a different person and running independently. A MOOC (massive open online course) seeks to get masses of people registered, knowing that a tiny fraction will complete it, while CE best practices focus on establishing effective learning in small online communities, and then potentially scale up from there by multiplying out. CEs aim to address the needs of online learners who want to:

- dig deeper, make "thicker" connections with other learners
- connect topics with their own interests
- participate for short periods of time
- learn without needing credits or badges

Currently, even the most high-profile MOOCs do not appear to be conducive to deep or thick inquiry. For example, while link-sharing is typical in "connectivist" or "cMOOCs", annotation and

Case Study: Collaborative Explorations 161

discussion of the contents is less common. By contrast, CEs are structured to elicit participants' thoughtful reflections and syntheses. The use of the internet for CEs, in contrast, is guided by two principles of online education (Taylor 2007).

- Use computers first and foremost to teach or learn things that are difficult to teach or learn with pedagogical approaches that are not based on computers

- Model computer use, at least initially, on known best practices for teaching/learning without computers.

Thus, CEs bring in participants from a distance, make rapid connections with informants or discussants outside the course, and contribute to evolving guides to materials and resources. At the same time, participants benefit from the support of instructors/facilitators and peers who they can trust, and integrate what they learn with their own personal, pedagogical, and professional development.

Example scenarios or "cases"

Connectivist MOOCs: Learning and collaboration, possibilities and limitations

The core faculty member of a graduate program at a public urban university wants help as they decide how to contribute to efforts at the university program to promote open digital education. It is clear that the emphasis will not be on xMOOCs, i.e., those designed for transmission of established knowledge, but on cMOOCs. In other words, the plan is to emphasize connectivist learning and community development emerges around, but may extend well beyond, the materials provided by the MOOC hosts (Morrison 2013; Taylor 2013). What is not yet clear about is just how learning works in cMOOCs. What are the possibilities and limitations of this educational strategy? How do they bear on themes like creativity, community, collaboration, and openness?

The program is especially interested in anticipating any undesirable consequences...

Science and policy that would improve responses to extreme climatic events

Recent and historical climate-related events shed light on the social impact of emergency plans, investment in and maintenance of infrastructure, as well as investment in reconstruction. Policy makers, from the local level up, can learn from the experiences of others and prepare for future crises. The question for this case is how to get political authorities and political groups—which might be anywhere from the town level to the international, from the elected to the voluntary—interested in learning about how best to respond to extreme climatic events. Changes might take place at the level of policy, budget, organization, and so on. It should even be possible to engage people who do not buy into the idea of human-induced climate change—after all, whatever the cause, extreme climatic events have to be dealt with....

The structure

Independent of the topic, we've found the following common structure useful for our online CEs. *Before the first live session*: Participants review the scenario, the expectations and mechanics, join a special-purpose Google+ community and get set up technically for the hangouts.

Session 1: *Participants getting to know each other*. After freewriting to clarify thoughts and hopes, followed by a quick check-in, participants take 5 minutes each to tell the story of how they came to be a person who would be interested to participate in a Collaborative Exploration on the scenario. Other participants note connections with the speaker and possible ways to extend their interests, sharing these using an online form.

Between-session work: Spend at least 90 minutes on inquiries related to the case, posting about this to google+ community for the

Case Study: Collaborative Explorations   163

CE, and reviewing the posts of others.

Session 2: *Clarify thinking and inquiries.* Freewriting on one's thoughts about the case, followed by a check-in, then turn-taking "dialogue process" to clarify what participants are thinking about their inquiries into the case. Session finishes with gathering and sharing thoughts using an online form.

Between-session work: Spend at least 90 minutes (a) on inquiries related to the case and (b) preparing a work-in-progress presentation.

Session 3: *Work-in-progress presentations.* 5 minutes for each participant, with "plus-delta" feedback given by everyone on each presentation. *Between-session work*: Digest the feedback on one's presentation and revise it into a self-standing product (i.e., one understandable without spoken narration).

Session 4: *Taking Stock.* Use same format as for session 2 to explore participants' thinking about (a) how the Collaborative Exploration contributed to the topic (the tangible goal) and to the experiential goal, as well as (b) how to extend what has emerged during the CE.

After session 4 (optional): Participants share on a public Google+ community not only the products they have prepared, but also reflections on the Collaborative Exploration process.

How to make sense of what happens in CEs

(Re-)engagement with oneself as an avid learner and inquirer in CEs is made possible by the combination of:

- Processes and tools used for inquiry, dialogue, reflection, and collaboration;

- Connections made among the diverse participants who bring to bear diverse interests, skills, knowledge, experience, and aspirations; and

```
         Connections
          ↙      ↘
Processes  ⇄  Contributions to Topic
```

Figure 1. Triad of aspects of Collaborative Exploration

Contributions from the participants to the topics laid out in scenarios

The hope is that through experiencing a (re-)engagement with learning, participants will subsequently transfer experience with this triad (Figure 1) into their own inquiries and teaching-learning interactions, the ways that they support inquiries of others; other practices of critical intellectual exchange and cooperation; and that they will be more prepared to challenge the barriers to learning that are often associated with expertise, location, time, gender, race, class, or age.

Acknowledgements

The comments of Jeremy Szteiter and the contributions of the participants of the 2013 Collaborative Explorations have helped in the preparation of this article.

Part II (by Teryl Cartwright).

As a May graduate of the Master's program in Critical and Creative Thinking (CCT) at UMass Boston, I owe my gratitude to Professors Peter Taylor and Jeremy Szteiter for inviting me to informally continue my education less than a month later. It is a tribute to them that I would then take four consecutive CEs without stopping. They can best share how to run a CE, but as a "student," it is how to creatively take a CE that inspires what I'd like to share.

CASE STUDY: COLLABORATIVE EXPLORATIONS   165

June 2013 CE: Scaffolding Creative Learning

I was grateful participants took the time to post links and ideas to support my inquiries, yet something else intrigued me about the potential of Collaborative Exploration. Luanne Witkowski, an artist and one of the CCT instructors, took our ideas and made a diagram incorporating our scaffolding concepts together; she changed her own original drawing to include all of ours. I wanted to pay forward and back my learning too, so I combined the ideas of all the participants, adapted and taught a lesson outside the CE and then shared the results. From this jumping into someone else's scaffolding, I went into even more experimental learning in the next CE.

July 2013 CE: Design in Critical Thinking

In a second CE, I took the title literally and developed a design IN critical thinking. To try out my triangle tangent thinking model, during a lesson on leadership in church, I suddenly stopped teaching a classroom of older professional adults halfway in and asked them to participate in "design as you go" curriculum—by taking over the class.

Since I wanted to be fair, along with my lesson outline I had already given them a supposed "icebreaker" activity that they could teach from, although they also had the option of my continued teaching. Results? My triangle drawing works as a lesson plan; the class took the tangent, but surprisingly, I wasn't just relegated to moderator, it became a true co-facilitation, a model of change at the midpoint for both the individual and community in the choices and direction.

September 2013 CE: Everyone Can Think Creatively

This CE had to be commended for its participants humoring my project and allowing the exploration of testing a CE itself. Was it possible to be a Creative Failure in a Creativity CE? To evaluate "Creative Failure in a Creativity CE,"

I used a simple test. If creative success (unknowingly given by my CE community) was a product both "novel AND useful," any post without a comment was a failure ("not useful") to my readers. Any post that a reader commented was similar to something else already done was "useful," but not novel. Failure had me posting again. Did I mention what nice people these were when they didn't know what I was doing?

It would have been easy for them to ignore my continued posting, yet the community of a CE cannot be praised enough. They were supportive of me and finding academic colleagues who have a sense of humor is mercifully not novel, but extremely useful in this experience.

October 2013 CE: Stories to Scaffold Creative Learning

In this CE I gave myself the challenge of indirect teaching. Could I be a story "shower", not teller? I took concepts important to me about teaching with story, yet also tried to leave space for others' interpretations. Ironically, in some ways creative failure continued—again I was not as helpful as I had wished.

This CE also had a twist—no hero stories allowed, so my creative and personal stories had to be ambiguous or use other connecting structures based on the participants' preferences. It was interesting which stories worked best—fiction worked more with humor, real experience worked if I shared about someone other than myself and other kinds worked with visuals.Collaborative Explorations provide a safe space for the joint learning and teaching to occur.

The diversity blends well into a community that is curious, courageous and creative. Although I have my M.A. as the first completely online CCT student, I found almost a face-to-face learning "feel" in their deeply connected CE community as well. It does require time, openness and commitment to each other during the intense focus together on a topic. Yet seeing where the participant-directed 'design as you go' curriculum ends up is worth investing in and sharing with others. After all, there are many other ways still out there to try out CEs.

Postscript. I also ran a CE for the Susquehanna Conference of the UMC for 10 days, working with a group of professionals exploring a call into ordained ministry. Going in cold, I had to work harder to do community building without the Google hangout meetings and recommend their inclusion to increase the comfort level and participation of the group members.

Resources

Further examples of CE scenarios can be viewed at HTTP://CCT.WIKISPACES.COM/CET. Recommended readings listed at the end of the book convey some of the sources for the CE processes. Ideas about possible extensions of CEs can be viewed in the full prospectus at HTTP://CCT.WIKISPACES.COM/CEP.

References

1. Morrison, D. (2013). "A TALE OF TWO MOOCS @ COURSERA: DIVIDED BY PEDAGOGY".

2. Taylor, P. J. (2007) "Guidelines for ensuring that educational technologies are used only when there is significant pedagogical benefit," International Journal of Arts and Sciences, 2 (1): 26-29, 2007 (adapted from HTTP://BIT.LY/ETGUIDE).

3. Taylor, P. J. (2013). "SUPPORTING CHANGE IN CREATIVE LEARNING".

Part VII

Cooperation

CHAPTER 21

INTRODUCTION TO COOPERATION: CO-FACILITATION

Author: Maria Arenas, with contributions by Charlie Danoff

Facilitation is a process of helping groups work cooperatively and effectively. Facilitation can be particularly helpful for individuals who, based on a certain level of insecurity or inexperience, tend to lurk rather than participate. At the same time, it in peeragogy, a facilitator isn't necessarily an "authority": rather, facilitation work is done in service to the group and the group dialogue and process. For example, a facilitator may simply "hold space" for the group, by setting up a meeting or a regular series of discussions.

Co-facilitating in peer-to-peer learning

Co-facilitation can be found in collaborations between two or more people who need each other to complete a task, for example, learn about a given subject, author a technical report, solve a problem, or conduct research Dee Fink writes that "in this process, there has to be some kind of change in the learner. No change, no learning" [1]. Significant learning requires that there be some kind of lasting change that is important in terms of the learner's life; in peeragogy, one way to measure the effectiveness of co-facilitation is to look for a change in the peer group.

Co-facilitation roles can be found in groups/teams like basketball, health, Alcoholics Anonymous, spiritual groups, etc. For example, self-help groups are composed of people who gather to share common problems and experiences associated with a particular problem, condition, illness, or personal circumstance. There are some further commonalities across different settings. Commenting on the work of Carl Rogers:

Godfrey Barrett-Lennard: The educational situation which most effectively promotes significant learning is one in which (1) threat to the self of the learner is reduced a minimum, and (2) differentiated perception of the field of experience is facilitated. [2]

Part of the facilitator's role is to create a safe place for learning to take place; but they should also challenge the participants.

John Heron: Too much hierarchical control, and participants become passive and dependent or hostile and resistant. They wane in self-direction, which is the core of all learning. Too much cooperative guidance may degenerate into a subtle kind of nurturing oppression, and may deny the group the benefits of totally autonomous learning. Too much autonomy for participants and laissez-faire on your part, and they may wallow in ignorance, misconception, and chaos. [3]

Co-facilitating discussion forums

If peers are preparing a forum discussion, here are some ideas from "THE COMMUNITY TOOL BOX", that can be helpful as guidelines:

- Explain the importance of collaborative group work and make it a requirement.
- Establish how you will communicate in the forum.
- Be aware of mutual blind spots in facilitating and observing others.
- Watch out for different rhythms of intervention.

Co-facilitating wiki workflows

A good place to begin for any group of co-facilitators working with a wiki are Wikipedia's famous "5 Pillars."

- Wikipedia is an encyclopedia.

- Wikipedia writes articles from a neutral point-of-view.

- Wikipedia is free content that anyone can edit, use, modify, and distribute.

- Editors should interact with each other in a respectful and civil manner.

- Wikipedia does not have firm rules.

Co-facilitating live sessions

Learning experiences in live sessions are described in the article LEARNING RE-IMAGINED: PARTICIPATORY, PEER, GLOBAL, ONLINE by Howard Rheingold, and many of these points are revisited in the handbook section on real-time tools. But we want to emphasize one point here:

> **Howard Rheingold**: Remember you came together with your peers to accomplish something, not to discuss an agenda or play with online tools; keep everything as easily accessible as possible to ensure you realize your goals.

References

1. Fink, L. D (2003). *Creating significant learning experiences: An integrated approach to designing college courses.* John Wiley & Sons.

2. Barrett-Lennard, G. T. (1998). *Carl Rogers' Helping System: Journey & Substance.* Sage.

3. Heron, J. (1999). *The complete facilitator's handbook.* London: Kogan Page.

CHAPTER 22

THE WORKSCAPE, A LEARNING PLATFORM FOR CORPORATIONS

Cultivating a results-oriented peer-learning program in a corporate learning ecosystem involves a few tweaks of the approach and tools we discussed in relation to more open, diverse networks.

The Workscape, a platform for learning

Formal learning takes place in classrooms; informal learning happens in *workscapes.* A workscape is a learning ecology. As the environment of learning, a workscape includes the workplace. In fact, a workscape has no boundaries. No two workscapes are alike. Your workscape may include being coached on giving effective presentations, calling the help desk for an explanation, and researching an industry on the Net. My workscape could include participating in a community of field technicians, looking things up on a search engine, and living in France for three months. Developing a platform to support informal learning is analogous to landscaping a garden. A major component of informal learning is natural learning, the notion of treating people as organisms in nature. The people are free-range learners. Our role is to protect their environment, provide nutrients for growth, and let nature take its course. A landscape designer's goal is to conceptualize a harmonious, unified, pleasing garden that makes the most of the site at hand. A workscape designer's goal is to create a learning environment that increases the organization's longevity and health and the individual's happiness and well-being. Gardeners don't control plants; managers don't control people. Gardeners and managers have influence but not absolute authority. They can't make a plant fit into the landscape or a person fit into a team. In an ideal Workscape, workers can easily find the people and information they need, learning is fluid and new ideas flow freely, corporate citizens live and work by the organization's values, people know the best way to get things done, workers spend more time creating value than handling exceptions, and everyone finds their work challenging and fulfilling.

The technical infrastructure of the Workscape

When an organization is improving its Workscape, looking at consumer applications is a good way to think about what's required. Ask net-savvy younger workers how they would like to learn new skills, and they bring up the features they enjoy in other services:

- Personalize my experience and make recommendations, like Amazon.

- Make it easy for me to connect with friends, like Facebook.

- Keep me in touch with colleagues and associates in other companies, as on LinkedIn.

- Persistent reputations, as at eBay, so you can trust who you're collaborating with.

- Multiple access options, like a bank that offers access by ATM, the Web, phone, or human tellers.

- Don't overload me. Let me learn from YouTube, an FAQ, or linking to an expert.

- Show me what's hot, like Reddit, Digg, MetaFilter, or Fark do.

- Give me single sign-on, like using my Facebook profile to access multiple applications.

- Let me choose and subscribe to streams of information I'm interested in, like BoingBoing, LifeHacker or Huffpost.

The Workscape

- Provide a single, simple, all-in-one interface, like that provided by Google for search.

- Help me learn from a community of kindred spirits, like SlashDot, Reddit, and MetaFilter.

- Give me a way to voice my opinions and show my personality, as on my blog.

- Show me what others are interested in, as with social bookmarks like Diigo and Delicious.

- Make it easy to share photos and video, as on Flickr and YouTube.

- Leverage "the wisdom of crowds," as when I pose a question to my followers on Twitter or Facebook.

- Enable users to rate content, like "Favoriting" an item on Facebook or +!ing is on Google or YouTube.

Some of those consumer applications are simple to replicate in-house. Others are not. You can't afford to replicate Facebook or Google behind your firewall. That said, there are lots of applications you can implement at reasonable cost. Be skeptical if your collaborative infrastructure that doesn't include these minimal functions:

Profiles - for locating and contacting people with the right skills and background. Profile should contain photo, position, location, email address, expertise (tagged so it's searchable). IBM's Blue Pages profiles include how to reach you (noting whether you're online now), reporting chain (boss, boss's boss, etc.), link to your blog and bookmarks, people in your network, links to documents you frequently share, members of your network.

Activity stream - for monitoring the organization pulse in real time, sharing what you're doing, being referred to useful information, asking for help, accelerating the flow of news and information, and keeping up with change

Wikis - for writing collaboratively, eliminating multiple versions of documents, keeping information out in the open, eliminating unnecessary email, and sharing responsibility for updates and error correction

Virtual meetings - to make it easy to meet online. Minimum feature set: shared screen, shared white board, text chat, video of participants. Bonus features: persistent meeting room (your office online), avatars.

Blogs - for narrating your work, maintaining your digital reputation, recording accomplishments, documenting expert knowledge, showing people what you're up to so they can help out

Bookmarks - to facilitate searching for links to information, discover what sources other people are following, locate experts

Mobile access - Half of America's workforce sometimes works away from the office. Smart phones are surpassing PCs for connecting to networks for access and participation. Phones post most Tweets than computers. Google designs its apps for mobile before porting them to PCs.

Social network - for online conversation, connecting with people, and all of the above functions.

Conclusion

Learning used to focus on what was in an individual's head. The individual took the test, got the degree, or earned the certificate. The new learning focuses on what it takes to do the job right. The workplace is an open-book exam. What worker doesn't have a cell phone and an Internet connection? Using personal information pipelines to get help from colleagues and the Internet to access the world's information is encouraged. Besides, it's probably the team that must perform, not a single individual. Thirty years ago, three-quarters of what a worker need to do the job was stored in her head; now it's less than 10%.

CHAPTER 23

PARTICIPATION

Methods of managing projects, including learning projects, range from more formal and structured to casual and unstructured. As a facilitator, you'll see your peeragogy community constantly adjust, as it seeks an equilibrium between order and chaos, ideally allowing everyone to be involved at their own pace without losing focus, and in such a manner that the collective can deliver.

Hey you, stop this train!

For teachers reading this, and wondering how to use peeragogy to improve participation in their classrooms, it's really quite simple: reframe the educational vision using peeragogical eyes. Recast the classroom as a community of people who learn together, the teacher as facilitator, and the curriculum as a starting point that can be used to organize and trigger community engagement. However, just because it's simple doesn't mean it's easy! Whatever your day job may be, consider: how well do the various groups you participate in work together – even when the members ostensibly share a common purpose? Sometimes things tick along nicely, and, presumably, sometimes it's excruciating. What's your role in all of this? How do *you* participate?

Guidelines for participation

- Accept that some people want to watch what is going on before jumping in. This doesn't mean you have to keep them hanging around forever. After a while, you may un-enroll people who don't add any value to the community. In our Peeragogy project, we've asked people to explicitly re-enroll several times. Most do renew; some leave.

- Accept that people may only contribute a little: if this contribution is good it will add value to the whole.

- Understand that you can not impose strict deadlines on volunteers; adjust targets accordingly.

- Let your work be "open" in the sense described in Wikipedia's NEUTRAL POINT OF VIEW policy.

- Give roles to participants and define some "energy centers" who will take the lead on specific items in the project.

- Organize regular face-to-face or online meetings to talk about progress and what's needed in upcoming days/weeks.

- Ask participants to be clear about when they will be ready to deliver their contributions.

- Have clear deadlines, but allow contributions that come in after the deadline – in general, be flexible.

- Add a newcomer section on your online platform to help new arrivals get started. Seasoned participants are often eager to serve as mentors.

Participation

When we think about project management in an organization, we often relate to well-established tools and processes. For example, we can use the PROJECT MANAGEMENT BODY OF KNOWLEDGE (PM-BOK) as a standard. For the Project Management Institute (PMI) and many workers, these standards are seen as the key to project success. In classical project management, tasks and deadlines are clearly defined. We will, for example, use PROGRAM EVALUATION AND REVIEW TECHNIC (PERT) to analyze and represent tasks. We often represent the project schedule using a GANTT CHART. Those are just two of the project management tools that illustrate how "mainstream" project management rests firmly on an engineering background. In these very structured projects, each actor is expected to work exactly as planned and to deliver his part of the work on time; every individual delay can potentially lead to a collective delay.

Peeragogy projects may be, naturally, a bit different from other settings, although we can potentially reuse both formal and informal methods of organization. For example, unlike a typical wiki – or classroom – peeragogy projects often expect to break the 90/9/1 RULE. Keep in mind that some participants may not contribute all the time – but one really good idea can be a major contribution. See the anti-pattern "Misunderstanding Power" for some further reflections on these matters.

How are we doing? If we take our Google+ Community have contributed to the handbook as the basic population, then as of January 2014, over 4% have contributed – pretty good. However, we have yet to reach a contribution profile like 70/20/10.

It's important to remember that – especially in a volunteer organization – no one can "make" other people participate, and that all the lists of things to do are for nought if no one steps in to do the work. For this reason, if anything is going to happen, what's needed are *realistic* estimates of available work effort. Finally, in closing this section, we want to emphasize that measures of participation offer only a very rough proxy for measures of learning, although the two are clearly related.

CHAPTER 24

NEW DESIGNS FOR CO-WORKING AND CO-LEARNING

Author: Joe Corneli

The word "learning" does not adequately capture what it means to figure out the "*for what purpose or reason*" dimension that is essential for a peeragogical endeavor. Interpersonal exchange and collaboration to develop and pursue common goals goes further than "learning" or "working" in their mainstream definitions. This article will look at examples drawn from Linux, Wikipedia, and my own work on PlanetMath, with a few surprises along the way, leading us to new ways of thinking about how to do co-design when build systems for peer learning and peer production.

Co-working as the flip side of convening

Linus Torvalds: The first mistake is thinking that you can throw things out there and ask people to help. That's not how it works. You make it public, and then you assume that you'll have to do all the work, and ask people to come up with suggestions of what you should do, not what they should do. Maybe they'll start helping eventually, but you should start off with the assumption that you're going to be the one maintaining it and ready to do all the work. The other thing–and it's kind of related–that people seem to get wrong is to think that the code they write is what matters. No, even if you wrote 100% of the code, and even if you are the best programmer in the world and will never need any help with the project at all, the thing that really matters is the users of the code. The code itself is unimportant; the project is only as useful as people actually find it.

In fact, we can think of contributors as a special class of "user" with a real time investment in the way the project works. We typically cannot "Tom Sawyer" ourselves into leisure or ease just because we manage to work collaboratively, or just because we have found people with some common interests. And yet, in the right setting, many people do want to contribute! For example, on "Wikipedia, the encyclopedia anyone can edit" (as of 2011) AS MANY AS 80,000 visitors make 5 or more edits per month.

This is interesting to compare with the EMPIRICAL FACT that (as of 2006) "over 50% of all the edits are done by just .7% of the users... 24 people...and in fact the most active 2%, which is 1400 people, have done 73.4% of all the edits." Similar numbers apply to other peer production communities.

'AIN'T THAT WORK?'

A little theory

In many natural systems, things are not distributed equally, and it is not atypical for e.g. 20% of the population to control 80% of the wealth (or, as we saw, for 2% of the users to do nearly 80% of the edits). Many, many systems work like this, so maybe there's a good reason for it.

Let's think about it in terms of "coordination" as understood by the late Elinor Ostrom. She talked about "local solutions for local problems". By definition, such geographically-based coordination requires close proximity. What does "close" mean? If we think about homogeneous space, it just means that we draw a circle (or sphere) around where we are, and the radius of this circle (resp. sphere) is small.

An interesting MATHEMATICAL FACT is that as the dimension grows, the volume of the sphere gets "thinner", so the radius must increase to capture the same d-dimensional volume when d grows! In other words, the more different factors impact on a given issue, the less likely there are to be small scale, self-contained, "local problems" or "local solutions" in the first place.

As a network or service provider grows (like a MOOC as opposed to a Collaborative Exploration, for example), they typically build many weak ties, with a few strong ties that hold it all together. Google is happy to serve everyone's web requests – but they can't have just anyone walking in off the street and connecting devices their network in Mountain View.

By the way, the 2006 article on Wikipedia quoted above was written by Aaron Swartz ("over 50% of all the edits are done by... 24 people", etc.), who achieved considerable NOTORIETY for doing something similar with MIT's network. His is a particularly sad case of one person acting alone and drawing significant ire from institutions and governments; we could contrast Aaron Swartz, the individual, with the peer-to-peer infrastructures like the ones that run PirateBay, which have proved much harder to stop.

Co-working: what is an institution?

As idealists, we would love to be able to create systems that are both powerful and humane. Some may reflect with a type of sentimental fondness on completely mythical economic systems in which a "dedicated individual could rise to the top through dint of effort." Well-articulated systems like this *do* exist, however: natural languages, for example, are so expressive and adaptive that most sentences have never been said before. A well-articulated system lends itself to "local solutions to local problems" – but in the linguistics case, this is only because all words are not created equal.

> **Dr Seuss**: My brothers read a little bit. Little words like 'If' and 'It.' My father can read big words, too, Like CONSTANTINOPLE and TIMBUKTU.

We could go on here to talk about Coase's theory of the firm, and Benkler's theory of "COASE'S PENGUIN". We might continue QUOTING from Aaron Swartz. But we will not get so deeply into that here: you can explore it on your own! For now, it is enough to say that an institution is a bit like a language. This will help us a lot in the next section.

Designing a platform for peer learning

> PLANETMATH *is a virtual community which aims to help make mathematical knowledge more accessible.*

In my PhD thesis [1], I talk about my work to turn this long-running website, which since 2001 had focused on building a mathematics encyclopedia, into a peer produced peer learning environment. The picture below shows the basic idea. We would retain all of the old activities related to authoring, reviewing, and discussing encyclopedia articles, but we would also add a bunch of new features having to do with mathmatical problem solving, an activity that is suitable for mathematical beginners.

Old objects   New objects

(diagram: Old objects side shows boxes labeled "article", "article", "comment", "comment", "article", "correction"; New objects side shows dotted boxes labeled "profile", "problem", "goal", "problem", "solution", "review")

My first translation of that sketch into a basic interaction design was as follows. People can continue to add articles to PlanetMath's encyclopedia: they can connect one article to another either by making one article the "parent" of another ($A \leftarrow A$), or, more typically, via an inline link, ℓ. Like in the old system, users can discuss any object ($X \leftarrow T$), but now there is more structure: *problems* can be connected to articles ($A \leftarrow P$) and *solutions* can be connected to problems ($P \leftarrow S$). Instead of explicitly modeling "goals," the idea I came up with was that problems and articles could be organized into "collections," the same way that videos are organized into playlists on YouTube, and that the user would get encouraging feedback as they work their way through the problems in a given collection. I described a few other types of objects and interactions that were not present in the above sketch, like questions and answers, groups, and the ability to change the "type" of certain contributed objects. This table summarizes the overall design.

Context	Feedback	Quality	Structure	Heuristic
$A \leftarrow A$ $A \xleftarrow{\ell} A$	$X \leftarrow T$ $S \leftarrow R$	$X \leftarrow Q$ $A \leftarrow C$	$A \leftarrow P \leftarrow S$ $L \leftarrow A, P$ $M \leftarrow A$ $Q \leftarrow A$	$G \leftarrow U$ $S \leftarrow H$ $Q, T \rightarrow C, W, P$
A article ℓ link X object	T post S solution R review	Q question C correction	P problem L collection M classific.	G group U user W request H heuristic

The next step was to do a complete overhaul of PlanetMath's software system, to build something that could actually *do* all of that. After deploying the system and doing some studies with PlanetMath users (described in the handbook section on Researching Peeragogy), I realized the design summarized above was not complete. Note that this is very much along the lines of what Linus Torvalds said above: I did the design, and me and a small group of collaborators with their own vested interests built the system, then we put it out there to get more ideas from users. Here the updated table, coming out of the co-design process.

Context	Feedback	Quality	Structure	Heuristic
$A \leftarrow A$	$X \leftarrow T$	$X \leftarrow Q$	$A \leftarrow P \leftarrow J \leftarrow S$	$G \leftarrow U$
$A \xleftarrow{\ell} A$	$S \leftarrow R$	$A \leftarrow C$	$L \leftarrow A, P$	$S \leftarrow H$
$X \rightarrow X$	$X \rightarrow X^{\sharp}$	$X \rightarrow X'$	$M \leftarrow A$	$Q, T \rightarrow C, W, P$
		$X \vDash X^{*}$	$Q \leftarrow A$	$G \hookrightarrow E$
A article	T post	Q question	P problem	G group
ℓ link	S solution	C correction	L collection	U user
X object	R review		M classific.	W request
				H heuristic
X project	$\sharp$ update	$'$ fork	J conjecture	E ephemera
		$\star$ outcome		

The main thing that was missing from the earlier design was the idea of a *project*. From interviewing users, it became clear to me that it would be helpful to think of every object as being part of at least one project: everything should have someone looking after it! Importantly, getting back to the very beginning of this article, each project can define its own purpose for existing. Here's how I put it in my thesis:

> *Actions and artifacts are embedded with projects, which can be modeled in terms of informal user experience and formal system features. Project updates can be modeled with a language of fundamental actions. Projects themselves model their outcomes, and are made "viable" by features that connect to the motivations and ambitions of potential participants.*

The key point to make about these tables is that they describe a "grammar" for the kinds of things that can be done on PlanetMath. In the updated grammar, projects are like sentences. The language can be extended further, and I hope this will happen in further study. In particular, we need to understand more about how the "sub-language" of project updates (which connects to our Roadmap pattern).

Another way to think about things

The five categories I used above (Context, Engagement, Quality, Structure, and Heuristic) come from reflecting on the 5 paragogy principles, and comparing them with the 5 RULES FOR THE EVOLUTION OF COOPERATION that were developed by Martin Nowak [2]. The analogies between these two sets of five categories are not perfect, and this exercise was meant to inspire, rather than to constrain, thoughts on the learning/platform design. Nowak's formalism is meant to be general enough to describe many different kinds of collaboration: I'll review the key points below, and show how they inspired my thinking about PlanetMath. The broader reason why Nowak's work is so essential is that we already have theories of local collaboration (like Ostrom's, mentioned above): his five rules can act as "glue" that bring different local entities together. I hope you can use these ideas in your own design projects!

> In a "kin selection" regime, we cooperate with whomever (or whatever) is "related".

On PlanetMath, the most important senses of "relatedness" apply to elements of the subject domain: encyclopedia pages are linked together if the topics relate.

> In a "direct reciprocity" regime, we help those who help us.

One of the key legacy features of PlanetMath is that every object in the system is "discussable." This is the most easily graspable sort of peer interaction, direct feedback, starting a conversation.

> *In an "indirect reciprocity" regime, we are building something that may be useful later on – like a good reputation.*

An important legacy feature of PlanetMath is that, unlike Wikipedia, articles are not generally open to the public to edit: high-quality resources "emerge" from the mediated engagement of individuals in a peer review process.

> *In a "spatial selection" regime, we are again defining an "inside" and "outside."*

With the new system, we see that "an article without an attached problem" is not as practical as an article that has an attached problem; similarly, "a problem without a solution" is lacking something. This helps people see what's missing, and what remains to be done.

> *In a "group selection" regime, we are building "sets" of activities and patterns (milestones, roles) which can then act as selectors for behavior.*

Co-working requires people to be able to join groups, and it requires the groups to be able to structure their workflow. In some sense this is similar to an individual's work being structured by the use of heuristics. A person's choice to join this group instead of that one, is a basic social heuristic.

The discussion continues: Reliving the history of mathematics as a peeragogical game?

These notes have shown one approach to the design of spaces for learning and knowledge building. Although the article has focused on mathematics learning, similar reflections would apply to designing other sorts of learning spaces, for instance, to the continued development of the Peeragogy project itself! – and perhaps to the development of a new kind of institutions.

Doug Breitbart: It occurred to me that you could add a learning dimension to the site that sets up the history of math as a series of problems, proofs and theorems that, although already solved, could be re-cast as if not yet solved, and framed as current challenges which visitors could take on (clearly with links to the actual solutions, and deconstruction of how they were arrived at, when the visitor decides to throw in the towel).

Reference

1. Corneli, J. (2014). PEER PRODUCED PEER LEARNING: A MATHEMATICS CASE STUDY. Unpublished Ph. D. thesis. The Open University.

2. Nowak, M. (2006). FIVE RULES FOR THE EVOLUTION OF CO-OPERATION, *Science*.

CHAPTER 25

A CO-WORKING STORY

The board of a housing association needs to set a strategy that takes account of major changes in legislation, the UK benefits system and the availability of long term construction loans. Julian, eager to make use of his new-found peeragogical insights suggests an approach where individuals research specific factors and the team work together to draw out themes and strategic options. As a start he proposes that each board member researches an area of specific knowledge or interest.

Jim, the Chairman, identifies questions he wants to ask the Chairs of other Housing Associations. Pamela (a lawyer) agrees to do an analysis of the relevant legislation. Clare, the CEO, plans out a series of meetings with the local councils in the boroughs of interest to understand their reactions to the changes from central government. Jenny, the operations director, starts modelling the impact on occupancy from new benefits rules. Colin, the development director, re-purposes existing work on options for development sites to reflect different housing mixes on each site. Malcolm, the finance director, prepares a briefing on the new treasury landscape and the changing positions of major lenders.

Each member of the board documents their research in a private wiki. Julian facilitates some synchronous and asynchronous discussion to draw out themes in each area and map across the areas of interest. Malcolm, the FD, adapts his financial models to take different options as parameters. Clare refines the themes into a set of strategic options for the association, with associated financial modelling provided by Malcolm. Individual board members explore the options asynchronously before convening for an all-day meeting to confirm the strategy.

Part VIII

Assessment

CHAPTER 26

INTRODUCTION TO PEERAGOGICAL ASSESSMENT

Authors: Joe Corneli and David Preston

This article is about both assessment in peer learning and an exercise in assessment, as we put our strategy for assessment into practice by evaluating the Peeragogy Handbook itself.

Adapting strategies for learning assessment to the peer-learning context

In "EFFECTIVE GRADING: A TOOL FOR LEARNING AND ASSESSMENT," Barbara E. Walvoord and Virginia Johnson Anderson have outlined an approach to grading. They address three questions:

1. Who needs to know, and why?

2. Which data are collected?

3. How does the assessment body analyze data and present findings?

The authors suggest that institutions, departments, and assessment committees should begin with these simple questions and work from them towards anything more complex. These simple questions provide a way to understand - and assess - any strategy for assessment! For example, consider "formative assessment" (in other words, keeping track of how things are going). In this context, the answers to the questions above would be:

1. Teachers need to know about the way students are thinking about their work, so they can deliver better teaching.

2. Teachers gather a lot of these details on learning activities by "listening over the shoulders" of students.

3. Teachers apply analysis techniques that come from their training or experience – and they do not necessarily present their assessments to students directly, but rather, feed it back in the form of improved teaching.

This is very much a "teacher knows best" model! In order to do something like formative assessment among peers, we would have to make quite a few adjustments.

1. At least some of the project participants would have to know how other participants are thinking about their work as well as analyzing their own progress. We are then able to "deliver better teaching" and work together to problem-solve when difficulties arise.

2. It may be most convenient for each participant to take on a share of the work (e.g. by maintaining a "learning journal" which might be shared with other participants). This imposes a certain overhead, but as we remarked elsewhere, "meta-learning is a font of knowledge!" Outside of persistent self-reflection, details about others' learning can sometimes be abstracted from their contributions to the project ("learning analytics" is a whole topic unto itself).

3. If a participant in a "learning project" is bored, frustrated, feeling closed-minded, or for whatever other reason "not learning," then there is definitely a question. But for whom? For the person who isn't learning? For the collective as a whole? We may not have to ponder this conundrum for long: if we go back to the idea that "learning is adaptation," someone who is not learning in a given context will likely leave and find another context where they can learn more.

This is but one example of an assessment strategy: in addition to "formative assessment", "diagnostic" and "summative" strategies are also quite popular in mainstream education. The main purpose of this section has been to show that when the familiar roles from formal education devolve "to the people," the way assessment looks can change a lot. In the following section, we offer and begin to implement an assessment strategy for evaluating the peeragogy project as a whole.

Case study in peeragogical evaluation: the Peeragogy project itself

We can evaluate this project partly in terms of its main "deliverable," the Peeragogy Handbook (which you are now reading). In particular, we can ask: Is this handbook useful for its intended audience? If so, in what ways? If not, how can we adapt? The "intended audience" could potentially include anyone who is participating in a peer learning project, or who is thinking about starting one. We can also evaluate the learning experience that the co-creators of this handbook have had. Has working on this book been a useful experience for those involved? These are two very different questions, with two different targets for analysis – though the book's co-creators are also part of the "intended audience". Indeed, we might start by asking "how has working on this book been useful for us?"

A methodological interlude: "Follow the money"

The metrics for learning in corporations are business metrics based on financial data. Managers want to know: "Has the learning experience enhanced the workers' productivity? When people ask about the ROI of informal learning, ask them how they measure the ROI of formal learning. Test scores, grades, self-evaluations, attendance, and certifications prove nothing. The ROI of any form of learning is the value of changes in behavior divided by the cost of inducing the change. Like the tree falling over in the forest with no one to hear it, if there's no change in behavior over the long haul, no learning took place. ROI is in the mind of the beholder, in this case, the sponsor of the learning who is going to decide whether or not to continue investing.

Because the figure involves judgment, it's never going to be accurate to the first decimal place. Fortunately, it doesn't have to be. Ballpark numbers are solid enough for making decisions.

The process begins before the investment is made. What degree of change will the sponsor accept as worthy of reinvestment? How are we going to measure that? What's an adequate level of change? What's so low we'll have to adopt a different approach? How much of the change can we attribute to learning? You need to gain agreement on these things beforehand. Monday morning quarterbacking is not credible. It's counterproductive to assess learning immediately after it occurs. You can see if people are engaged or if they're complaining about getting lost, but you cannot assess what sticks until the forgetting curve has ravaged the learners' memories for a few months.

Interest also doesn't guarantee results in learning, though it helps. Without reinforcement, people forget most of what they learn in short order. It's beguiling to try to correlate the impact of learning with existing financial metrics like increased revenues or better customer service scores. Done on its own, this approach rarely works because learning is but one of many factors that influence results, even in the business world. Was today's success due to learning or the ad campaign or weak competition or the sales contest or something else?

The best way to assess how people learn is to ask them. How did you figure out how to do this? Who did you learn this from? How did that change your behavior? How can we make it better? How will you? Self-evaluation through reflective practice can build both metacognition and self-efficacy in individuals and groups.

Too time consuming? Not if you interview a representative sample. For example, interviewing less than 100 people out of 2000 yields an answer within 10% nineteen times out of twenty, a higher confidence level than most estimates in business. Interviewing 150 people will give you the right estimate 99% of the time.

Roadmaps in Peer Learning

We have identified several basic and more elaborated patterns that describe "the Peeragogy effect". These have shaped the way we think about things since. We think the central pattern is the Roadmap, which can apply at the individual level, as a personal learning plan, or at a project level. As we've indicated, sometimes people simply plan to see what happens: alternative versions of the Roadmap might be a compass, or even the ocean chart from the *Hunting of the Snark*. The roadmap may just be a North Star – or it may include detailed reasons "why," further exposition about the goal, indicators of progress, a section for future work, and so forth. Our initial roadmap for the project was the preliminaly outline of the handbook; as the handbook approached completion at the "2.0" level, we spun off additional goals into a new roadmap for a Peeragogy Accelerator. Additional patterns flesh out the project's properties in an open "agora" of possibilities. Unlike the ocean, our map retains traces of where we've been, and what we've learned. In an effort to document these "paths in the grass," we prepared a short survey for Peeragogy project participants. We asked people how they had participated (e.g., by signing up for access to the Social Media Classroom and mailing list, joining the Google+ Community, authoring articles, etc.) and what goals or interests motivated their participation. We asked them to describe the Peeragogy project itself in terms of its aims and to evaluate its progress over the first year of its existence. As another measure of "investment" in the project, we asked, with no strings attached, whether the respondent would consider donating to the Peeragogy project. This survey was circulated to 223 members of the Peeragogy Google+ community, as well as to the currently active members of the Peeragogy mailing list. The responses outlining the project's purpose ranged from the general: "How to make sense of learning in our complex times" - to much more specific:

> **Anonymous Survey Respondent 1**: Push education further, providing a toolbox and [techniques] to self-learners. In the peeragogy.org introduction page we assume that self-learners are self-motivated, that may be right but the Handbook can also help them to stay motivated, to motivate others and to face obstacles that may erode motivation.

Considering motivation as a key factor, it is interesting to observe how various understandings of the project's aims and its flaws intersected with personal motivations. For example, one respondent (who had only participated by joining the Google+ community) was: "[Seeking] [i]nformation on how to create and engage communities of interest with a shared aim of learning." More active participants justified their participation in terms of what they get out of taking an active role, for instance:

> **Anonymous Survey Respondent 2**: "Contributing to the project allows me to co-learn, share and co-write ideas with a colourful mix of great minds. Those ideas can be related to many fields, from communication, to technology, to psychology, to sociology, and more."

The most active participants justified their participation in terms of beliefs or a sense of mission:

> **Anonymous Survey Respondent 3**: "Currently we are witnessing many efforts to incorporate technology as an important tool for the learning process.

However, most of the initiatives are reduced to the technical aspect (apps, tools, social networks) without any theoretical or epistemological framework. Peeragogy is rooted in many theories of cooperation and leads to a deeper level of understanding about the role of technology in the learning process. I am convinced of the social nature of learning, so I participate in the project to learn and find new strategies to learn better with my students."

Or again:

Anonymous Survey Respondent 4: "I wanted to understand how "peer production" really works. Could we create a well-articulated system that helps people interested in peer production get their own goals accomplished, and that itself grows and learns? Peer production seems linked to learning and sharing - so I wanted to understand how that works."

They also expressed criticism of the project, implying that they may feel rather powerless to make the changes that would correct course:

Anonymous Survey Respondent 5: "Sometimes I wonder whether the project is not too much 'by education specialists for education specialists.' I have the feeling peer learning is happening anyway, and that teens are often amazingly good at it. Do they need 'learning experts' or 'books by learning experts' at all? Maybe they are the experts. Or at least, quite a few of them are."

Another respondent was more blunt:

Anonymous Survey Respondent 6: "What problems do you feel we are aiming to solve in the Peeragogy project? We seem to not be sure. How much progress did we make in the first year? Some... got stuck in theory."

But, again, it is not entirely clear how the project provides clear pathways for contributors to turn their frustrations into changed behavior or results. Additionally we need to be entirely clear that we are indeed paving new ground with our work. If there are proven peer learning methods out there we have not examined and included in our efforts, we need to find and address them. Peeragogy is not about reinventing the wheel. It is also not entirely clear whether excited new peers will find pathways to turn their excitement into shared products or process. For example, one respondent (who had only joined the Google+ community) had not yet introduced current, fascinating projects publicly:

> **Anonymous Survey Respondent 7**: "I joined the Google+ community because I am interested in developing peer to peer environments for my students to learn in. We are moving towards a community-based, place-based program where we partner with community orgs like our history museum for microhistory work, our local watershed community and farmer's markets for local environmental and food issues, etc. I would love for those local efforts working with adult mentors to combine with a peer network of other HS students in some kind of cMOOC or social media network."

Responses such as this highlight our need to make ourselves available to hear about exciting new projects from interested peers, simultaneously giving them easier avenues to share. Our work on developing a peeragogy accelerator in the next section is an attempt to address this situation.

Summary

We can reflect back on how this feedback bears on the main sections of this book with a few more selected quotes. These motivate further refinement to our strategies for working on this project, and help build a constructively-critical jumping off point for future projects that put peeragogy into action.

Cooperate *How can we build strong collaboration?* "A team is not a group of people who work together. A team is not a group of people who work together. A team is a group of people who trust each other."

Convene *How can we build a more practical focus?* "The insight that the project will thrive if people are working hard on their individual problems and sharing feedback on the process seems like the key thing going forward. This feels valuable and important."

Organize *How connect with newcomers and oldcomers?* "I just came on board a month ago. I am designing a self-organizing learning environment (SOLE) or PLE/PLN that I hope will help enable communities of life long learners to practice digital literacies."

Assess *How can we be effective and relevant?* "I am game to also explore ways attach peeragogy to spaces where funding can flow based on real need in communities."

Conclusion

We can estimate individual learning by examining the real problems solved by the individual. It makes sense to assess the way groups solve problems in a similar way. Solving real problems often happens very slowly, with lots of practice along the way. We've learned a lot about peer learning in this project, and the assessment above gives a serious look at what we've accomplished, and at how much is left.

CHAPTER 27

RESEARCHING PEERAGOGY

Author: Joe Corneli

If you have a research bent, by this point, you may be asking yourself questions like these: *How can we understand peer learning better? How can we do research "the peeragogical way"? How do we combine research and peer learning?* You may also be asking more technical methodological and instrumentation-level questions: *Do we have a good way to measure learning? Which activities and interventions have the biggest payoff?*

This chapter summarizes qualitative research I did on PlanetMath.org, using the pattern catalog, as part of my work for my PhD. In the course of the study, I developed 3 new patterns.

The first point to make is that although this research was informal, it is nevertheless (at least in my view) highly rigorous. This is because the pattern catalog is a relatively stable, socially agreed upon objct, though it is not fixed for all time. We can use it to help identify "known" patterns, but we can also extend it with new patterns – assuming that we can make an argument to explain why the new patterns are needed. The notion of patternfinding as a process related to, but distinct from abstraction is described by Richard Gabriel, who emphasizes that the "patterns and the social process for applying them are designed to produce organic order through piecemeal growth" ([1], p. 31).

We can use the rigorous-but-informal notion of an expanding pattern catalog to help address the high-level questions about peeragogical research mentioned above. The three new patterns I present here are: Frontend and Backend, Spanning Set, and Minimum Viable Project. These patterns are both an "outcome" of research in a real peer learning context – and also a reflection on peeragogical research methods. Like the other peeragogy patterns, they are tools you can use in your own work.

```
┌─────────┐      ┌─────────┐
│   Lab   │      │ Library │
└─────────┘      └─────────┘
           Quad
┌─────────┐      ┌─────────┐
│  Dorm   │      │  Forum  │
└─────────┘      └─────────┘
```

Map of a virtual campus

Study design

The study was based on interviews with users of a new software system that we deployed on PlanetMath.org. In the interviews, we covered a wide range issues, ranging from basic issues of usability all the way to "deep" issues about how people think about mathematics. In this project, I was interested not only in how people collaborate to solve mathematical problems, but how they think about "system level" issues. The design I had in mind is depicted in the figures below. The key idea is that patterns emerge as "paths in the grass", or "desire lines". The idea that learning design has emergent features is not itself new; see e.g. [2]. What's new here is a characterization of the key patterns for *doing* emergent design in a peer learning context.

Initial thematic analysis

Before describing the new patterns, I will briefly summarize the themes I identified in the interviews. This can serve as an overview of the current features and shortcomings of PlanetMath system for people who are not familiar with it.

```
┌─────────────┐           ┌─────────────┐
│  Context    │ Heart-    │ Nonlinearity│
│ [Articles]  │ beat      │ [Problems,  │
│             │           │  Solutions, │
│             │           │  Reviews]   │
└─────────────┘           └─────────────┘
    A specific   Roadmap        Divide
     project   [Groups & Collections]
┌─────────────┐           ┌─────────────┐
│Meta-learning│ Use or    │  Feedback   │
│ [Comments]  │ Make?     │[Corrections,│
│             │           │ Questions]  │
└─────────────┘           └─────────────┘
```

Peeragogy patterns as loci for "paths in the grass"

- **"Necessary but not sufficient".** Users identified a range of essential features, like a critical mass of other users to talk to.

- **"Nice to have".** It was also easy to identify a bunch of cool new "dream" features.

- **Challenges with writing mathematics.** PlanetMath uses LaTeX, which isn't entirely easy to learn (however, we could adapt the software to help new users get started).

- **Progressive problem solving.** The new PlanetMath contains problems and solutions, but no easy way to talk about conjectures. Users would like a better way to share and discuss work-in-progress.

- **Personal history, social constructivism.** Better features for tracking and, where appropriate, sharing, personal history would help users make sense of what's happening in the site.

- **Regulating learning in a social/mediated context.** Different users would look for different things to keep them on track (e.g. expert guidance, or a due "sense of urgency" in feedback from peers).

- **Comparison with roles in other contexts.** Many users expect a "service delivery" style that is not entirely consistent with the "open" production model used in a free/open, volunteer-driven project. We need to work more on responsiveness in every aspect of the project (keeping in mind that most participants are volunteers).

- **Concreteness as a criterion of quality.** "Knowing what you can do," both with the software and with the content, is important. On the content level, pictures help.

- **Personalization and localization.** The system has a practically unlimited potential for personalization, although many basic personalized interaction modes have not been built yet.

Pattern analysis

At the next level of analysis, the themes extracted above were further analysed in relationship to the peeragogy pattern catalog.

Frontend and Backend

Although mathematics is a relatively formal domain, many of the motivations for using PlanetMath map onto what Zimmerman and Campillo call informal problem solving [3]. Informal problems are are personally defined and possess openended boundary conditions, i.e., are situated within an "open world." I like thinking about this in terms of the way a car works. You can model the steering and drive system with classical mechanics. But you ultimately need to model the engine with statistical mechanics and chemistry. You get in a car and start driving and usually it works more or less the way you'd expect. This is how it works with other "formal" systems. You queue here, sign there, pay your fee, and it's all done. With informal systems, it's messier. Of course, the car's engine has a detailed diagram, and for a mechanic, it's just another "formal" system. And, yes, the streets at rush hour can get very messy. It's all relative. The broader point is that where ever it appears, "formal" is straightforward. In order to design a collaborative system, you want to bring in enough messiness to let new and unexpected features emerge – support for serendipity – but you also need to be aware of the user's experience. As another analogy, imagine a butcher shop. You want the user to be able to take away nice little packages of meat, you don't want them cutting up whole cows. Leave that to the pros. The idea of Frontend and Backend is related to the pattern of the "Newcomer" pattern, since typically one will not expect the user of a system to know how to, or to be motivated to, work with backend features of a system until they have mastered at least some of the frontend features. It would be rare to find an auto mechanic who did not know how to drive. David Cavallo wrote about an "engine culture" in rural Thailand, in which structurally open systems made some of the "backend" features of internal combustion engines a part of daily life [4]. In PlanetMath, we have an "open engine", but not necessarily an open engine culture (users expect a level of service provision). The Frontend and Backend pattern clearly lends itself to standard service provision, but it can also be part of paragogical activity. For example, sophisticated and committed users of the PlanetMath website could focus energy on supporting individual newcomers, by helping them develop a high-quality sub-site on their topic of interest. Such effort would simultaneously inform the development of backend features, and help raise the profile of the site as a whole. The pattern is in this way associated with Focusing on a Specific Project and with the Divide pattern.

Spanning Set

You may be able to get what you need without digging - but if you do need to dig, it would be very good to get some indication about which direction to dig in. At the content level, this might be achieved by using high-level "topic articles" as a map to the content. But there is another broader interpretation of this pattern that related to but distinct from Frontend and Backend - we call this the Spanning Set. In general, the Spanning Set might be made up of people, or media objects. In a standard course model, there is one central node, the teacher, who is responsible for all teaching and course communication. In large online courses, this model can be is scaled up:

> **Anonymous study participant**: [E]veryone's allocated a course tutor, who might take on just a half-dozen students - so, they're not the overall person in charge of the course, by any means.

Another version is the classical master/apprentice system, in which every apprentice is supervised by a certified master. In the typical online Q&A context, these roles are made distributed, and are better modeled by power laws than by formal gradations. A "spanning set" of peer tutors could help shift the exponent attached to the power law in massive courses. We can imagine a given discussion group of 100 persons that is divided according to the so-called 90/9/1 RULE, so that 90 lurk, 9 contribute a little, and 1 creates the content. This is what one might observe, for example, in a classroom with a lecture format. We could potentially shift the system by breaking the group up, so that each of the 9 contributors leads a small group of 10 persons, at which point, chances are good that some of the former lurkers would be converted into contributors. At a more semantic level, we can advance the five paragogical principles and their various analogues as a candidate description of the fundamental categories and relationships relevant to peer learning. In practice, principles can only provide the most visible "frontend", and an actual spanning set is comprised of emergent patterns. In PlanetMath, this would arise from combining several different features, like a "start menu" that shows what can be done with the site, a Heartbeat built of recurring meetings, and topic-level guides to content. (Note: as a project with an encyclopedic component, PlanetMath itself can be used to span and organize a significantly larger body of existing material.)

Minimum Viable Project

The Minimum Viable Product approach to software development is about putting something out there to see if the customer bites [5]. Another approach, related to the pattern we just discussed, is to make it clear what people can do with what's there and see if they engage. We might call this the Minimum Viable Project, an adjunct to the "Roadmap" pattern, and yet another interpretation of Focusing on a Specific Project. One way to strengthen the PlanetMath project as a whole would be to focus on support for individual projects. The front page of the website could be redesigned so that the top-level view of the site is project focused. Thus, instead of collecting all of the posts from across the site - or even all of the threads from across the site - the front page could collect succinct summary information on recently active projects, and list the number of active posts in each, after the model of Slashdot stories or StackExchange questions. For instance, each Mathematics Subject Classification could be designated as a "sub-project", but there could be many other cross-cutting or smaller-scale projects.

Summary

This chapter has used the approach suggested by Figure 2 to expand the peeragogy pattern language. It shows that the peeragogy pattern language provides a "meta-model" that can be used to develop emergent order relative to given boundary conditions. As new structure forms, this becomes part of the boundary conditions for future iterations. This method is a suitable form for a theory of peer learning and peer production in project-based and cross-project collaborations - a tool for conviviality in the sense of Ivan Illich. In other words, we're all in the same boat. The things that peer learners need in order to learn stuff in a peer produced setting are exactly the same things that designers and system builders need, too. And one concrete way to assess our collective learning is in terms of the growth and refinement of our pattern catalog.

Frontend and Backend
Principles and features

Minimum Viable Project
A Specific Project, Roadmap, Heartbeat, Divide, Use or Make

Spanning Set
Paths in the grass

Peeragogical emergent design: a tool for conviviality

References

1. Gabriel, R. (1996). Patterns of Software. Oxford University Press New York.

2. Luckin, R. (2010). Re-designing learning contexts: technology-rich, learner-centred ecologies. Routledge.

3. Zimmerman, B. J. & Campillo, M. (2003). Motivating self-regulated problem solvers. In J. Davidson & R. Sternberg (Eds.), The psychology of problem solving (pp. 233-262). Cambridge University Press New York, NY.

4. Cavallo, D. P. (2000). Technological Fluency and the Art of Motorcycle Maintenance: Emergent design of learning environments (Doctoral dissertation, Massachusetts Institute of Technology).

5. Ries, E. (2011). The Lean Startup: How today's entrepreneurs use continuous innovation to create radically successful businesses. Crown Pub.

Part IX

Technologies, Services, and Platforms

CHAPTER 28

INTRODUCTION TO TECHNOLOGIES FOR PEERAGOGY

Author: Gigi Johnson

It is tempting to bring a list of technologies out as a glorious cookbook. We need a 1/2 cup of group writing tools, 2 tsp. of social network elements, a thick slice of social bookmarking, and some sugar, then put it in the oven for 1 hour for 350 degrees.

We have created a broad features/functions list for Handbook readers to reflect upon and consider. The joy of this list is that you can consider alternatives for the way you communicate and work while you are planning the project, or can add in new elements to solve communications gaps or create new tools.

However, too many tools spoil the broth. In the writing of this Handbook, we found that out firsthand. We spent a lot of marvelous energy exploring different tools to collaborate, curate information, do research, tag resources, and adjudicate among all of our points of view. In looking at groups working with the various MOOCs, as another example, different groups of students often camp in different social media technologies to work.

In large courses, students often have to be pushed into various social media tools to "co-create" with great protest and lots of inertia. And finally, co-learning groups often come from very different backgrounds, ages, and stages of life, with very different tools embedded in their current lives. Do we have time for three more tools in our busy days? Do more tools help – or do they interfere with our work?

In this section, we'll share with you a few issues:

- What technologies are most useful in peer learning? What do we use them for? What features or functions help our co-learning process?

- How do we decide (a) as a group and (b) for the group on what tools we can use? Do we decide upfront, or grow as we go?

- How do we coach and scaffold each other on use of tools?

- How much do the tool choices impact the actual outcome of our learning project?

- What are the different roles that co-learners can take in co-teaching and co-coaching the technology affordances/assumptions in the project to make others' lives easier?

Keep in mind – your needs for tools, plus how the way the group uses them, will change as the co-learning project moves along. Technologies themselves tend to change rapidly. Are you willing to change tools during the project as your needs and users change, or do you plan to use a given tool set from the beginning to the end of your project?

Features and Considerations

We will begin below with a discussions of "features" and initial considerations, and then move to a broader "Choose Your Own Adventure"-style matrix of features leading to a wide variety of collaboration-based technology tools online.

Technologies and Features

As we will share in the extensive list below, there are abundant tools now available – both for free and for pay – to bring great features to our co-learning endeavors. It is tempting to grab a group of fancy tools and bring the group into a fairly complex tool environment to find the perfect combination of resources. The challenge: adult learners seek both comfort and context in our lives [1], [2]. In choosing tool "brands", we can ignore the features themselves and what we need as parts of the puzzle for learning. We also can have anxiety about our self-beliefs around computers and technology, which in turn can limit our abilities [3].

Before we get to brands and choices, it helps to ask a few questions about the learning goals and environments:

- What do we need as features, and at what stage of the learning process?

- What are we already comfortable with, individually and as a group?

- Do we want to stay with comfortable existing tools, or do we want to stretch, or both?

- What types of learners do we have in this group? Technologically advanced? Comfortable with basics?

- Do we want to invest the time to bring the whole group up to speed on tools? Do all the group members agree on this? Do we want to risk alienating members by making them invest time in new resources?

- We know that our use will migrate and adapt. Do we want to plan for adaptation? Observe it? Learn from it? Make that change intentional as we go?

Researchers over the years have heavily examined these questions of human, technology, and task fit in many arenas. HUMAN-COMPUTER INTERACTION researchers have looked at "fit" and "adaptive behavior," as well as how the tools can affect how the problem is presented by Te'eni [4]. Creativity support tools [5] have a whole line of design research, as has the field of COMPUTER-SUPPORTED COLLABORATIVE WORK SYSTEMS (CSCW). For co-learners and designers interested in the abundance in this space, we've added some additional links below. We here will make this a bit easier. For your co-learning environment, you may want to do one or two exercises in your decision planning:

What *features do you need*? Do you need collaboration? Graphic models? Places to work at the same time (synchronous)? Between meetings (asynchronous)? What are the group members *already using* as their personal learning platforms? It also makes sense to do an inventory about what the group already has as their learning platforms. I'm doing that with another learning group right now. People are much more comfortable – as we also have found in our co-creation of this Handbook – creating and co-learning in tools with which they already are comfortable. Members can be co-teachers to each other – as we have have – in new platforms. What *type of tools*, based on the features that we need, shall we start out with? Resnick *at al.* [6] looked at tools having:

- Low thresholds (easy to get people started)
- Wide walls (able to bring in lots of different situations and uses) and
- High ceilings (able to do complex tasks as the users and uses adapt and grow).

What are important features needed for co-creation and *working together*? In other pages above, we talk abundantly about roles and co-learning challenges. These issues also are not new; Dourish & Bellottii [7] for example, shared long-standing issues in computer-supportive collaborative work online about how we are aware of the information from others, passive vs. active generation of information about collaborators, etc. These challenges used to be "solved" by software designers in individual tools. Now that tools are open, abundant, and diverse, groups embrace these same challenges when choosing between online resources for co-learning.

Useful Uses and fancy Features of Technological Tools

From here, we will help you think about what might be possible, linking to features and solution ideas.

We start with ways to ask the key questions: What do you want to do and why? We will start with features organized around several different axes:

1. Time/Place,

2. Stages of Activities and Tasks,

3. Skill Building/Bloom's Taxonomy,

4. Use Cases, and

5. Learning Functions.

Each will link to pages that will prompt you with features, functionality, and technology tool ideas.

Time/Place

We can further break down tools into whether they create or distribute, or whether we can work simultaneously (synchronous) or at our own times (ascynchronous). To make elements of time and place more visual, Baecker [8] created a CSCW Matrix, bringing together time and place functions and needs. Some tools are synchronous, such as Google+ Hangouts, Blackboard Collaborate, and Adobe Connect, while others let us work asynchronously, such as wikis, forums, and Google Docs. We seem to be considering here mostly tools good for group work, but not for solo, while many others are much easier solo or in smaller groups.

	Same Time (Synchronous)	Different Time (Ascynronous)
Same Place (Colocated)	**Face-to-Face**: Display-focused (e.g., Smartboards)	**Ongoing Tasks**: Groupware, project management tools
Different Place (Remote)	**Remote Interaction**: Videoconference, IM, Chat, Virtual Worlds	**Communication & Coordination**: Email, bulletin boards, Wikis, blog, workflow tools

Stages of Activities and Tasks

Ben Shneiderman [5] has simplified the abundant models in this area (e.g., Couger and Cave) with a clear model of 4 general activities and 8 tasks in creation for individuals, which we can lean on as another framework for co-creation in co-learning.

Collect	**Relate**	**Create**	**Distribute**
Searching, Visualizing	Consulting Others	Thinking, Exploring, Composing, Reviewing	Disseminating

Tools and functions won't be clear cut between areas. For example, some tools are more focused on being generative, or for creating content. Wikis, Etherpad, Google docs, and others usually have a commenting/talk page element, yet generating content is the primary goal and discursive/consultative functions are in service of that. Some tools are discursive, or focused on working together for the creative element of "relating" above – Blackboard Collaborate, the social media class room forums, etc.

Skill Building (Cognitive, a la Bloom's Taxonomy, see below)

Given that we are exploring learning, we can look to Bloom's Taxonomy (revised, see [9]) for guidance as to how we can look at knowledge support. Starting at the bottom, we have:

- Remembering, as a base;
- Understanding,
- Applying,
- Analyzing,
- Evaluating, and then, at the top,
- Creating.

We could put "search" in the Remembering category above. Others contest that Search, done well, embraces most of the Bloom's elements above. Samantha Penney has created a BLOOM'S DIGITAL TAXONOMY PYRAMID infographic, describing tools for learning, which you may want to check out.

Use Cases (I want to....)

Technologies can be outlined according to the need they serve or use case they fulfill. Examples: If we need to 'curate', Pearl Trees is an option. To 'publish' or 'create', we can look to a wiki or wordpress. Other choices might be great in order to 'collaborate', etc.

One challenge is that tools are not that simple. As we look more closely at the technologies today, we need to reach more broadly to add multiple tags to them. For example Twitter can be used for "Convening a group," for "micro-blogging," for "research," etc.

- Collaborate with a Group
- Create Community
- Curate Information
- Research
- Publish Information
- Create Learning Activities
- Make Something

These plans get more complex, as you are making a group of decisions about tool functionality in order to choose what combination works for use cases. It may be most useful to use a concept map (a tech tool) to think about the needs and combinations that you would bring together to achieve each Use Case or Learning Module.

Technology Features/Functions

We have not made this easy! There are lots of moving elements and options here, none of them right for everything, and some of them fabulous for specific functions and needs. Some have the low thresholds but may not be broad in scope. Some are broad for many uses; others are specific task-oriented tools. That is some of the charm and frustration.

Weaving all of the above together, we have brought together a shared taxonomy for us to discuss and think about co-learning technology features and functions, which we present as an appendix below. This connects various technology features within an expanded version of Ben Shneiderman's creativity support tools framework. We've created this linked toolset with multiple tags, hopefully making it easier for you to evaluate which tool suits best the necessities of the group. Please consider this a starting point for your own connected exploration.

Weaving all of these frameworks together, we have brought together a shared taxonomy for us to discuss and think about co-learning technology features and functions. We have connected various technology features with an expanded version of Ben Shneiderman's creativity support tools framework for the linked resource guide. For convenience and to help keep it up to date, we're publishing this resource ON GOOGLE DOCS. We present an overview in an appendix.

References

1. Schein, E. H. (1997). *Organizational learning as cognitive re-definition: Coercive persuasion revisited.* Cambridge, MA: Society for Organizational Learning.

2. Schein, E. H. (2004). *Organizational culture and leadership.* San Francisco, CA: Jossey-Bass.

3. Compeau, D.R., & Higgins, C.A. (1995, June). Computer Self-Efficacy: Development of a Measure and Initial Test. *MIS Quarterly, 19,* (2), 189-211.

4. Te'eni, D. (2006). Designs that fit: An overview of fit conceptualizations in HCI. In *Human-Computer Interaction and Management Information Systems: Foundations,* edited by P. Zhang and D. Galletta, pp. 205-221, Armonk, NY: M.E. Sharpe.

5. Shneiderman, B. (2002). Creativity support tools. *Commun. ACM* 45, 10 (October 2002), 116-120.

6. Resnick, M, Myers, B, Nakakoji, K, Shneiderman, B, Pausch, R, Selker, T. & Eisenberg, M (2005). DESIGN PRINCIPLES FOR TOOLS TO SUPPORT CREATIVE THINKING. *Institute for Software Research.* Paper 816.

7. Dourish, P. & Bellotti, V. (1992). Awareness and coordination in shared workspaces. In *Proceedings of the 1992 ACM conference on Computer-supported cooperative work* (CSCW '92). ACM, New York, NY, USA, 107-114.

8. Baecker, R., GRUDIN, J., BUXTON, W., & GREENBERG, & (eds.) (1995): *Readings in Human-Computer Interaction: Toward the Year 2000.* New York, NY: Morgan Kaufmann Publishers

9. Anderson, L. W., & Krathwohl, D. R. (Eds.). (2001). *A taxonomy for learning, teaching and assessing: A revision of Bloom's Taxonomy of educational objectives: Complete edition.* New York, NY: Longman.

Appendix: Features and Functions

Activities & Tasks

Planning/Designing

- Communicating
- Deciding and Creating Alternatives

Collect/Share

- Searching
- Visualizing

Relate

- Consulting Others from the Outside

Communication

- Connecting with Others in the Group

Co-Create

- Thinking (Free Association)
- Exploring
- Composing
- Reviewing

Distribute/Action

- Disseminating

Feedback

- Listening

Features & Functions

- Convening a group
- Planning a course/structure (assembling a syllabus, designing a learning activity)
- Designing self-assessment (group and individual)
- Setting individual and group goals
- Brainstorming
- Visualizing

- Search
- Social Bookmarking
- Creating/Finding Taxonomies (shared keywords, domain-based keywords)
- Programming Toolsets
- Collaborative reading
- Collaborative note-taking
- Curation Tools
- Gathering information (e.g., capturing audio, video, text)
- Surveys and Questionnaires

- Qualitative research
- Quantitative research

- Project Planning - Scheduling
- Voice/Video Conferencing Services
- Group Email / Forum Messaging Services
- File Sharing Service (cloud based)
- Screen Capturing and Screen Casting
- Presentation and Document Sharing

- Learning Management Systems
- Document Collaboration and Editing
- Visualizing Information for analysis and synthesis (concept maps, data visualization)

- Publishing Platforms (traditional publishing, social media/sharing distribution)
- Visualization (for presentation)

- Social Monitoring

CHAPTER 29

FORUMS

Author: Howard Rheingold

Forums are web-based communication media that enable groups of people to conduct organized multimedia discussions about multiple topics over a period of time. Selecting the right kind of platform for forum conversations is important, as is know-how about facilitating ongoing conversations online. Forums can be a powerful co-learning tool for people who may have never met face-to-face and could be located in different time zones, but who share an interest in co-learning. Asynchronous media such as forums (or simple email distribution lists or GOOGLE DOCS) can be an important part of a co-learning toolkit that also includes synchronous media from face-to-face meetups to GOOGLE+ HANGOUTS or webinars via BLACKBOARD COLLABORATE, ADOBE CONNECT, or the open source webconferencing tool, BIG BLUE BUTTON (discussed a little later in the handbook).

What is a forum and why should a group use it?

A forum, also known as a message board, BBS, threaded discussion, or conferencing system, affords asynchronous, many-to-many, multimedia discussions for large groups of people over a period of time. That means that people can read and write their parts of the discussion on their own schedule, that everyone in a group can communicate with everyone else, and that graphics, sounds, and videos can accompany text. The best forums index discussion threads by topic, title, tag, date,and/or author and also keep track of which threads and entries (also known as posts) each logged-in participant has already read, making it possible to click on a "show me all the new posts and threads" link each time a participant logs in. This particular form of conversational medium meets the need for organizing conversations after they reach a certain level of complexity. For example, if twenty people want to discuss five subjects over ten days, and each person makes one comment on each subject every day, that makes for one thousand messages in each participant's mailbox. On email lists, when the conversation drifts from the original topic, the subject line usually does not change, so it makes it difficult to find particular discussions later.

Forums make possible a new kind of group discussion that unfolds over days, weeks, and months, in a variety of media. While blogs are primarily about individual voice, forms can be seen as the voice of a group. The best forum threads are not serial collections of individual essays, but constitute a kind of discourse where the discussion becomes more than the sum of its individual posts. Each participant takes into account what others have said, builds on previous posts, poses and answers questions of others, summarize, distill, and concludes.

This short piece on GUIDELINES FOR DISCUSSION BOARD WRITINGis useful, as is this short piece on SHAPING A CULTURE OF CONVERSATION. Lively forums with substantial conversation can glue together the disparate parts of a peeragogy group – the sometimes geographically dispersed participants, texts, synchronous chats, blogs, wikis and other co-learning tools and elements. Forum conversations are an art in themselves and forums for learning communities are a specific genre. Reading the resources linked here – and communicating about them – can help any peeragogy group get its forums off to a good start

How to start fruitful forum discussions:

In most contexts, starting a forum with a topic thread for introductions tends to foster the sense of community needed for valuable conversations. THIS SHORT PIECE ON HOW TO HOST GOOD CONVERSATIONS ONLINEoffers general advice. In addition to introductions, it is often helpful to start a topic thread about which new topic threads to create – when everybody has the power to start a new thread and not everybody knows how forums work, a confusing duplication of conversations can result, so it can be most useful to make the selection of new topic threads a group exercise. A topic thread to ask questions about how to use the forum can prevent a proliferation of duplicate questions. It helps to begin a forum with a few topic threads that invite participation in the context of the group's shared interest "Who is your favorite photographer" for a group of photographers, for example, or "evolution of human intelligence" for a group interested in evolution and/or human intelligence. Ask questions, invite candidate responses to a challenge, make a provocative statement and ask for reactions.

Whether or not you use a rubric for assessing individual participants' forum posts, this guide to HOW FORUM POSTS ARE EVALUATED by one professor can help convey the difference between a good and a poor forum conversation:

4 Points - The posting(s) integrates multiple viewpoints and weaves both class readings and other participants' postings into their discussion of the subject.

3 Points - The posting(s) builds upon the ideas of another participant or two, and digs deeper into the question(s) posed by the instructor.

2 Points - A single posting that does not interact with or incorporate the ideas of other participants' comments.

1 Point - A simple "me too" comment that neither expands the conversation nor demonstrates any degree of reflection by the student.

0 Points - No comment.

Selecting a forum platform

- You don't want a forum for discussions among two or three people; you do want a forum for discussions among half a dozen or five thousand people.

- You don't want a forum for exchanges of short duration (an hour, a day or two) among any number of people; you do want a forum for ongoing conversations that can continue for months.

- You don't want a forum if blogs with comment threads will do – blogs with comments afford group discourse, but is not easily indexed and discourse gets complicated with more than a dozen or so bloggers and commenters.

If you do want to select a platform for forum discourse, you will want to decide whether you have the technical expertise available to install the software on your own server or whether you want to look for a hosted solution. Cost is an issue.

Fortunately, an online forum maven by the name of DAVID WOOLEY has been keeping an up-to-date list of available software and services for more than a decade:

- FORUM SOFTWARE FOR THE WEB

- FORUM AND MESSAGE BOARD HOSTING SERVICES

These 2003 SUGGESTIONS ON HOW TO CHOOSE A FORUM by Howard Rheingold can be helpful. If blogs with comments afford a kind of networked individualistic discourse, and video conferencing emulates face-to-face meeting, forums can be seen as a channel for expression of the group voice. When people react to and build on each other's comments, they can learn to act as a collective intelligence as well as a collection of individuals who are communicating in order to learn.

CHAPTER 30

WIKI

Author: Régis Barondeau

In the context of P2P-learning, a wiki platform can be a useful and powerful collaboration tool. This section will help you understand what a wiki is and what it is not, why you should use it, how to choose a wiki engine and finally how you could use it in a P2P context. Some examples of P2P-learning projects run on wikis will help you see the potential of the tool.

What is a wiki?

For WARD CUNNINGHAM father of the wiki, "a wiki is a freely expandable collection of interlinked Web 'pages', a hypertext system for storing and modifying information - a database, where each page is easily editable by any user with a forms-capable Web browser client" [1].

According to Wikipedia : "a wiki is a website whose users can add, modify, or delete its content via a web browser using a simplified markup language or a rich-text editor" [2].

You can watch this CommonCraft video WIKI IN PLAIN ENGLISH to better understand what a wiki is.

What differentiates the wiki from other co-editing tools?

The previous definitions show that a wiki is a "website," in other words it is composed of pages that are connected together by hyperlinks.In additiont every authorized person (not all wikis are totally open like Wikipedia) can edit the pages from a web browser, reducing time and space constrains. In case one saves a mistake or for any other reason would like to go back to a previous version, a feature called "history" allows users to see previous versions and to roll back any of them. This version history allows also to compare versions avoiding the cluttered of the "commentaries rainbow" we are used too in popular Word processors. For example if you work on a wiki page, and come back later on, you will be able to catch up by comparing your last version with the lastest version of someone else.

Tools like GOOGLE DOCS or ETHERPAD are design to enable co-editing on a single document. This can be seen as a "wiki way" of working on a document as it is web based and includes versioning. But it is not a wiki because a single document is not a website. Those tools offer realtime collaboration which wikis do not and are so far easier to use for beginners as they work in WYSIWYG mode, which many wikis do not support. However, the advanced features WIKI MARKUP LANGUAGE make it a more powerful tool. In summary, tools like Googles Docs or Etherpad are a great way to quickly collaborate (synchronously, asynchronously, or a mixture of both) on a single document for free, with a low barrier to entry and no technical support. (Note that Etherpad does have a "wiki-links" plugin that can allow it to be used in a more wiki-like way; HACKPAD is another real-time editing tool that prominently features linking – and it claims to be "the best wiki ever".)

Using a real wiki engine is more interesting for bigger projects and allows a huge number of users to collaborate on the same platform. A wiki reduces the coordination complication as e-mails exchanges are no more needed to coordinate a project. On the other hand it can help us deal with complexity ([3], [4]) especially if you put basic simple rules in place like the Wikipedia's NEUTRAL POINT OF VIEW to allow every participant to share her or his ideas.

Going back to the continuum we talked about before, some tools like Moodle, SharePoint, WordPress, Drupal or others have build in wiki features. Those features can be good but will typically not be as good for wiki-building purposes as a well-developed special-purpose wiki engine. In other words, those tools main focus is not the wiki, which is only a secondary feature. When you choose a real wiki engine like MEDIAWIKI, TIKI, FOSWIKI, etc., the wiki will be your platform, not a feature of it. For example if you start a wiki activity in a Moodle course, this wiki will be only visible to a specific group of students and searchable only to those students. On the other hand if your learning platform is a wiki, the whole platform will be searchable to all members regarding their permissions. We are not saying here that a wiki is better than other tools but if you need a wiki engine to address your needs you may consider going with a strong wiki engine rather than a "micro-wiki" engine embedded in an other tool.

Why use a wiki?

Those are the main reasons you should consider a wiki for your peer learning projects :

- To reduce coordination complication by having a central and always up to date place to store your content. You will reduce e-mail usage drastically, and have access to your content from everywhere using any operating system.

- To keep track of the evolution of your project and be able to view or roll back any previous version of a wiki page using the history feature.

- To make links between wiki pages to connect ideas and people but also make links to external URL's. This last possibility is very handy to cite your sources.

- To deal with complexity. As a wiki allows anyone to contribute, if you set some easy rules like Wikipedia's NPOV (Neutral Point of View), you will be able to catch more complexity as you will allow everyone to express his or her opinion. Wikis also integrate a forum or comment feature that will help you solve editing conflicts.

- To deal with work in progress. A wiki is a great tool to capture an on going work.

- To support transparency by letting every members of the community see what others are doing.

- To support a network structure as a wiki is by essence an horizontal tool.

Using hyperlinks, you can...

Gérard Ayache: "...jump by a single click from one network node to another, from a computer to another, from one piece of information to another, from one universe to another, from one brain to another." (Translated from [5].)

How to choose a wiki engine?

You will find more than a hundred different wiki engines.

The first main distinction is between open source ones that are free to download and commercial ones you will have to pay for. You will find powerful engines on both sides open source and commercial. Sometimes the open source ones look less polished at first sight but are backed by a strong community and offer a lot of customization possibilities. The commercial are sold like a package, they are nicely presented but often they offer less customization on the user side and additional feature or custom made tools will cost you an extra fee.

The second distinction that we can make is between wiki farms and self-hosted wikis. The WIKI FARM is a hosting service you can find for both open source or commercial wikis. The goal of those farms is to simplify the hosting of individual wikis. If you don't want to choose a wiki farm hosting, you will have to host the wiki on your own server. This will give you more latitude and data privacy but will require more technical skills and cost you maintenance fees.

The WIKIMATRIX web site will help you choose the best wiki for your needs. It allows you to compare the features of more than a hundred wiki engines. HERE is the top ten list of the best wiki engines by Ward Cunningham.

How can a wiki be useful in a peeragogy project?

A wiki is a good tool collaborative projects and a specially suited for work in progress as you can easily track changes using the history, compare those version and if necessary roll back a previous versions. In other words, nothing gets lost.

Here are some ideas about how to use a wiki in a peeragogy project :

- **Use a wiki as your learning platform**. It can also support MASSIVE OPEN ONLINE COURSES (MOOCs). A wiki will help you organize your LEARNING CONTEXT. You can choose to give access to your wiki only to the project participants or open it to the public like WIKIPEDIA. Using hyperlinking, you will operationalize the theory of CONNECTIVISM by connecting nodes together. As a learning platform wikis are powerful because you can easily see what others are doing, share with them, get inspired, merge ideas or link to ideas. In other words, it creates emulation between learners. For additional ressources about wiki in education follow this DIIGO LINK.

- **Manage your peeragogy project**. A wiki is an excellent tool for project collaboration. Above all, the wiki can be a central place for peer learners to write or link to content. Even if you use several technologies to run your project as we did to write this handbook, at the end of the day, all the content can be centralized on a wiki using direct writing on wiki pages or hyperlinks. This way members can access the content from anywhere and from any device connected to the internet using any platform or application and they will always see the most recent version while being able to browse through the versions history to understand what has changed since their last visit.

- **Publish your project**. As a wiki is a website you can easily use it to show your work to the world. Regarding web design, don't forget that a wiki can look way better than a Wikipedia page if you customize it

Examples of peeragogy projects run on wikis

APPROPEDIA is a wiki site for collaborative solutions in SUSTAINABILITY, POVERTY reduction and INTERNATIONAL DEVELOPMENT through the use of sound PRINCIPLES and APPROPRIATE TECHNOLOGY and the sharing of wisdom and PROJECT information. The site is open to stakeholders to find, create and improve scalable and adaptable solutions.

TEAHOUSE is a peeragogy project run on a wiki that gives newcomers a place to learn about Wikipedia culture and get feedback from experienced Wikipedians.

What are the best practices when using a wiki?

- **Cofacilitation** – help each other learn, help each other administer

- **Self-election** – enable people to choose what they want to work on, at their own pace, in their own way

- **Communication** – use comment threads and talk pages to discuss wiki changes

- **Documenting changes** – most wikis enable editors to write very brief descriptions of their edits

- **Rules** – keep rules at a minimum level to avoid chaos without constraining creativity

- **Fun** – make it fun for people to contribute

References

1. Leuf, Bo, et Ward, Cunningham. 2001. The Wiki way : quick collaboration on the Web. Boston: Addison-Wesley, xxiii, 435 p. p.14

2. WIKI on Wikipedia

3. Andrus, Calvin D. 2005. TOWARD A COMPLEX ADAPTATIVE INTELLIGENCE COMMUNITY - THE WIKI AND THE BLOG. Studies in Intelligence. vol. 49, no 3. Online :

4. Barondeau, Régis. 2010. LA GESTION DE PROJET CROISE LE WIKI. École des Sciences de la Gestion, Université du Québec à Montréal, 180 pp.

5. Ayache, Gérard. 2008. Homo sapiens 2.0 : introduction à une histoire naturelle de l'hyperinformation. Paris: Milo, 284 p. p.179

CHAPTER 31

REAL-TIME MEETINGS

Author: Howard Rheingold

Summary

Web services that enable broadband-connected learners to communicate in real time via audio, video, slides, whiteboards, chat, and screen-sharing enable learning groups to add some of the audio-visual dimensions familiar from synchronous face-to-face communication to otherwise asynchronous platforms such as forums, blogs, and wikis. This article includes resources for finding and evaluating appropriate for-free or for-fee platforms, tips on participative activities for real-time meetings, and suggestions for blending real-time and asynchronous media.

Real-time meeting media

The *Peeragogy Handbook* was conceived and constructed by a group of people on four continents who had not met and had not known about each other before we began meeting online. The process involves asynchronous media, including forums, wikis, social bookmarking groups, and Wordpress, but it probably would never have cohered into a group capable of collective action if it had not been for the real-time meetings where we were able to see each other's faces, hear each other's voices, use a whiteboard as an anonymous agenda-generator, exchange links in chat, show each other examples through screen-sharing. Together, the asynchronous and real-time media enabled us to begin to see ourselves as an effective group. We used both real-time and asynchronous tools to work out processes for creating, refining, and publishing the Handbook, to divide labor, decide on platforms and processes, to collaboratively compose and edit articles, and to design and add graphical and video elements. In particular, we used the BLACKBOARD COLLABORATE platform, a web-service that enables up to 50 people at a time to meet in a multimedia, recordable, meeting room for around $500/year. We've experimented with other paid platforms, such as ADOBE CONNECT (about the same price as Collaborate), and when we meet in groups of ten or less, we often use the free and recordable GOOGLE+ HANGOUT service. Smaller groups also use SKYPE or free telephone conferencing services. MUMBLE is an open source audio-only tool that is popular with gamers. We're watching the development of BIG BLUE BUTTON, a free and open-source real-time meeting platform, as it develops the full suite of tools that are currently only available for a fee. Dozens of other free, ad-supported and/or freemium web-conferencing systems such as BIG MARKER and DIM-DIM can be found in lists like HOWARD RHEINGOLD's and ROBIN GOOD's. Free phone conferencing services provide another technological "lowest common denominator": some provide a few extras like downloadable recordings.

Features of real-time meeting platforms

There are many free services for chat, screen-sharing, whiteboards, and video conferencing, but combining all these components in separate panes of the same screen (preferably) or as separate tabs of a browser can have a powerful synchronizing and harmonizing effect on the group. The features to look for in meeting platforms include:

Audio and video: Choose platforms that enable voice-over-internet-protocol (VOIP) and easy ways for participants to configure their microphones and speakers. Today's webcams, together with adequate lighting and a broadband connection, enable a number of people to be visible at the same time. In Blackboard Collaborate, the person who is speaking at a given moment is visible in the largest video pane, while other participants are available in smaller video windows. Audio and video convey much more of a human dimension than text communications alone. A group of people who have seen and heard each other online are able to work together via asynchronous media such as forums and wikis more effectively. Online face-to-face meetings are often the best way for a group to argue constructively and decide on critical issues. Forums and email are comparatively bad choices for distributed decison-making.

Slide pushing: The best platforms will convert .ppt or .pdf files for sequential display. With the addition of text chat, annotations to slides, and the ability to "raise your hand" or interrupt with your voice, an online lecture can be a more multidimensional experience than even a highly discursive in-person lecture.

Text chat: As a backchannel, a means of quickly exchanging links to relevant resources, a channel for collaborative note-taking, a way of communicating with the lecturer and with other participants, text chat adds a particularly useful dimension to real-time peeragogical meetings – especially when the division of labor is explicitly agreed upon in advance. We've found that even in meetings that use the real-time collaborative editor ETHERPAD for collaborative note taking, participants may gravitate toward the built-in chat box for discussion.

Screen sharing: The ability of participants to show each other what is on their screens becomes especially important in peer learning, where we all have some things to show each other.

Web tours: An alternative to screen-sharing is the ability to display the same web page(s) to all participants by entering URLs.

Interactive whiteboards: A shared space that enables participants to enter text, drawings, shapes, colors, to move and resize media, and to import graphic content – especially if it allows anonymous actions – can foster the feeling of participating in a collective intelligence. Collaborative anonymous mind-mapping of the discussion is one technique to try with whiteboards. The whiteboard can also be used to generate an emergent agenda for an "un-meeting".

Configuring Google+ Hangout - a free alternative for up to 10 people

For up to 10 people, each equipped with a webcam, microphone, and broadband connection, GOOGLE+ HANGOUT can provide high-quality audio-video conferencing. By enabling the text-chat feature and adding Google Docs (text documents, presentations, or spreadsheets), screensharing, and SketchUp (whiteboard), it is possible to emulate most of what the commercial services offer. Adobe Connect and Blackboard Collaborate currently have the user-interface advantage of displaying chat, video, whiteboard/slides as resizable panes on one screen; at present, the free Google services can provide a powerful extension of the basic audio-video platform, but participants have to shift between different tabs or windows in the browser. Note that it is possible to STREAM A HANGOUT AND RECORD IT TO YOUTUBE, again at no cost to the user. We've used this tool extensively in the Peeragogy project.

Suggestions for real-time meetings

In the nine online courses I have facilitated, the emphasis on co-learning encouraged participants to suggest and shape active roles during real-time meetings. By creating and taking on roles, and shifting from role to role, participants engage in a kind of collective learning about collective learning which can be as pleasurable as well as useful. Typically we first brainstorm, then analyze, then organize and present the knowledge that we discover, construct, and ultimately convey together.

Roles for participants in real-time meetings

- **Searchers:** search the web for references mentioned during the session and other resources relevant to the discussion, and publish the URLs in the text chat

- **Contextualizers:** add two or three sentences of contextual description for each URL

- **Summarizers:** note main points made through text chat.

- **Lexicographers:** identify and collaboratively define words and phrases on a wiki page.

- **Mappers:** keep track of top level and secondary level categories and help the group mindmapping exercise at the end of the session.

- **Curators:** compile the summaries, links to the lexicon and mindmaps, contextualized resources, on a single wiki page.

- **Emergent Agendas:** using the whiteboard for anonymous nomination and preference polling for agenda items, with voice, video, and text-chat channels for discussing nominations, a group can quickly set its own agenda for the real-time session.

The Paragogical Action Review

Charlie Danoff and Joe Corneli slightly modified the US Army's "After Action Review" into a technique for evaluating peer learning as it happens. The five steps in the "PAR" are:

1. Review what was supposed to happen

2. Establish what is happening

3. Determine what's right and wrong with what we are doing

4. What did we learn or change?

5. What else should we change going forward?

Participants can run through these steps during live meetings to reassess the medium, the readings, the group dynamics, or any other choices that have learning relevance. The focus in the PAR is on change: as such, it provides a simple way to help implement the "double loop learning" described Chris Argris [1].

Reference

1. Argyris, Chris. "Teaching smart people how to learn." Harvard Business Review, 69.3, 1991.

Part X

Resources

CHAPTER 32

HOW TO GET INVOLVED IN THE PEERAGOGY PROJECT

This page is for people who want to help develop/improve this handhook.

If you want to get involved, write to HOWARD RHEINGOLD *at* HOWARD@RHEINGOLD.COM.

Illustrations by AMANDA LYONS.

Hello and welcome!

The peeragogy project was kicked off around the time of HOWARD RHEINGOLD's January 23, 2012 REGENTS LECTURE at UC Berkeley on *Social Media and Peer Learning: From Mediated Pedagogy to Peeragogy*. We have put together a handbook about peer learning: you're reading it – maybe on OUR WEBSITE, or in your hammock with the beverage of your choice and our PRINT ON DEMAND paperback. Or maybe you grabbed our FREE PDF or some other remixed version in some other format or flavor from some other place (which would be cool!).

But: there's still more work to be done. We created this page because you might be interested in getting involved in improving the book or furthering the project in other ways. If so, we're happy to have you aboard!

What you do here is largely up to you. Asking questions is actually extremely helpful: there's almost always someone in our GOOGLE+ COMMUNITY who would be happy to try to answer them, or refer you to someone else who can. Or just poke around the public pages on peeragogy.org and leave a comment or two. Better still, find an area where you feel knowledgeable – or are willing to learn – and start writing (or filming, dancing, drawing, building, etc.).

The goal we have in mind for our book is for it be a useful guide to peer learning! To achieve that goal we have in mind multiple opportunities for peers to contribute:

- Once we get to know you a little bit we'll be happy to give you a login on peeragogy.org and you can start editing and improving this.

- You can go right ahead and post some links to relevant resources, either in comments here, or in the G+ or SMC.

- Write the text for a new sub-section (this page was once "new" – but it's been revised many times by now!).

- We're particularly interested in case studies about Peeragogy in Action!

- Organize a team to tackle a larger section or topic.

- Make a video (like these on our YouTube Channel),

- Take notes of live meetings, or grow concept maps,

- Organize a newsletter for your group or the whole team,

- Add general purpose bookmarks to this Diigo group, or post comments and editorial notes about peeragogy.org in this one; and

How to get involved

- Discuss peer learning matters and this handbook informally with us and with others!

It's up to you. Instead of worrying too much about the rules, join our conversations, take advantage of the digital memory of the forum to rewind the conversation all the way to the beginning (if you want to go that far), listen in for a little bit if you want to, and jump in whenever you're ready. We won't know what you're up to until you speak up. You can have a look at the outstanding tasks and teams that are listed on THIS GOOGLE DOC: our roadmap is a useful shared resource too. You can add to these at any time.

We regularly use Google+, Google Hangouts, forums, and email to communicate asynchronously and pretty much continuously. We also meet irregularly as a group for synchronous audio-video sessions. Further details about all these methods of communication can be found below.

In short: here's how it works:

Questions?

If you have questions, that's good! Use Google+ or the forums, post a comment on peeragogy.org, email the team energy center if you know who that is, or email HOWARD@RHEINGOLD.COM.

CHAPTER 33

PEERAGOGY IN ACTION

We have been writing the missing manual for peer-produced peer learning - the "Peeragogy Handbook" (peeragogy.org). Throughout the building of this work, we, ourselves peer learners in this quest, have been mindful of these four questions:

1. *How does a motivated group of self-learners choose a subject or skill to learn?*

2. *How can this group identify and select the best learning resources about that topic?*

3. *How will these learners identify and select the appropriate technology and communications tools and platforms to accomplish their learning goal?*

4. *What does the group need to know about learning theory and practice to put together a successful peer-learning program?*

It is clear to us that the techniques of peer production that have built and continue to improve *Wikipedia* and GNU/Linux have yet to fully demonstrate their power in education. We believe that the *Peeragogy Handbook* can help change that by building a distributed community of peer learners/educators, and a strongly vetted collection of best practices. Our project complements others' work on sites like Wikiversity and P2PU, and builds upon understandings that have developed informally in distributed communities of hobbyists and professionals, as well as in (and beyond) the classrooms of generations of passionate educators. Here, we present Peeragogy in Action, a project guide in four parts. Each part relates to one or more sections of our handbook, and suggests activities to try while you explore peer learning. These activities are designed for flexible use by widely distributed groups, collaborating via a light-weight infrastructure. Participants may be educators, community organizers, designers, hackers, dancers, students, seasoned peeragogues, or first-timers. The guide should be useful for groups who want to build a strong collaboration, as well as to facilitators or theorists who want to hone their practice or approach. Together, we will use our various talents to build effective methods and models for peer produced peer learning. Let's get started!

Setting the initial challenge and building a framework for accountability among participants is an important starting point.

Activity – Come up with a plan for your work and an agreement, or informal contract, for your group. You can use the suggestions in this guide as a starting point, but your first task is to revise the plan to suit your needs. It might be helpful to ask: What are you interested in learning? What is your primary intended outcome? What problem do you hope to solve? How collaborative does your project need to be? How will the participants' expertise in the topic vary? What sort of support will you and other participants require? What problems won't you solve?

Technology – Familiarize yourself with the collaboration tools you intend to use (e.g. Wordpress, Git and LaTeX, YouTube, GIMP, a public wiki, a private forum, or something else) and create a first post, edit, or video introducing yourself and your project(s) to others in the worldwide peeragogy community.

Suggested Resources – The Peeragogy Handbook, parts I ('Introduction') and II ('Peer Learning'). You may also want to work through a short lesson called IMPLEMENTING PARAGOGY, from the early days before the Peeragogy project was convened. For a succinct theoretical treatment, please refer to our literature review, which we have adapted into a WIKIPEDIA PAGE.

Further Reading – Boud, D. and Lee, A. (2005). *'Peer learning' as pedagogic discourse for research education.* Studies in Higher Education, 30(5):501–516.

Observations from the Peeragogy project – We had a fairly weak project structure at the outset, which yielded mixed results. One participant said: "I definitely think I do better when presented with a framework or scaffold to use for participation or content development." Yet the same person wrote with enthusiasm about models of entrepreneurship, saying she was "freed of the requirement or need for an entrepreneurial visionary." In short,

Other people can support you in achieving your goal and make the work more fun too.

Activity – Write an invitation to someone who can help as a co-facilitator on your project. Clarify what you hope to learn from them and what your project has to offer. Helpful questions to consider as you think about who to invite: What resources are available or missing? What do you already have that you can build on? How will you find the necessary resources? Who else is interested in these kinds of challenges? Go through the these questions again when you have a small group, and come up with a list of more people you'd like to invite or consult with as the project progresses.

Technology – Identify tools that could potentially be useful during the project, even if it's new to you. Start learning how to use them. Connect with people in other locales who share similar interests or know the tools.

Suggested resources – The Peeragogy Handbook, parts V ('Convening a Group') and VI ('Organizing a Learning Context').

Recommended Reading – Schmidt, J. Philipp. (2009). Commons-Based Peer Production and education. Free Culture Research Workshop Harvard University, 23 October 2009.

Observations from the Peeragogy project – We used a strategy of "open enrollment." New people were welcome to join the project at any time. We also encouraged people to either stay involved or withdraw; several times over the first year, we required participants to explicitly reaffirm interest in order to stay registered in the forum and mailing list.

Solidifying your work plan and learning strategy together with concrete measures for 'success' can move the project forward significantly.

Activity – Distill your ideas by writing an essay, making visual sketches, or creating a short video to communicate the unique plans for organization and evaluation that your group will use. By this time, you should have identified which aspects of the project need to be refined or expanded. Dive in!

Technology – Take time to mentor others or be mentored by someone, meeting up in person or online. Pair up with someone else and share knowledge together about one or more tools. You can discuss some of the difficulties that you've encountered, or teach a beginner some tricks.

Suggested resources – The Peeragogy Handbook, parts VII ('Co-Facilitation and Co-Working'), VIII ('Assessment'), and part IV ('Patterns, Use cases, and Examples').

Recommended reading – Argyris, Chris. "Teaching smart people how to learn." Harvard Business Review 69.3 (1991); and, Gersick, Connie J.G. "Time and transition in work teams: Toward a new model of group development." Academy of Management Journal 31.1 (1988): 9-41.

Observations from the Peeragogy project – Perhaps one of the most important roles in the Peeragogy project was the role of the 'Wrapper', who prepared and circulated weekly summaries of forum activity. This helped people stay informed about what was happening in the project even if they didn't have time to read the forums. We've also found that small groups of people who arrange their own meetings are often the most productive.

Wrap up the project with a critical assessment of progress and directions for future work. Share any changes to this syllabus that you think would be useful for future peeragogues!

Activity – Identify the main obstacles you encountered. What are some goals you were not able to accomplish yet? Did you foresee these challenges at the outset? How did this project resemble or differ from others you've worked on? How would you do things differently in future projects? What would you like to tackle next?

Writing – Communicate your reflection case. Prepare a short written or multimedia essay, dealing with your experiences in this course. Share the results by posting it where others in the broader Peeragogy project can find it.

'Extra credit' – Contribute back to one of the other organisations or projects that helped you on this peeragogical journey. Think about what you have to offer. Is it a bug fix, a constructive critique, pictures, translation help, PR, wiki-gnoming or making a cake? Make it something special, and people will remember you and thank you for it.

Suggested resources – The Peeragogy Handbook, parts IX ('Technologies, Services, and Platforms') and X ('Resources').

Recommended reading – Stallman, Richard. "WHY SOFTWARE SHOULD BE FREE" (1992).

Observations from the Peeragogy project – When we were deciding how to license our work, we decided to use CC0, emphasizing 're-usability' and hoping that other people would come and remix the handbook. At the moment, we're still waiting to see the first remix edition, but we're confident that it will come along in due course. Maybe you'll be the one who makes it!

Micro-Case Study: The Peeragogy Project, Year 1

Since its conception in early 2012, the Peeragogy Project has collected over 3700 comments in our discussion forum, and over 200 pages of expository text in the handbook. It has given contributors a new way of thinking about things together. However, the project has not had the levels of engagement that should be possible, given the technology available, the global interest in improving education, and the number of thoughtful participants who expressed interest. We hope that the handbook and this accompanying syllabus will provide a seed for a new phase of learning, with many new contributors and new ideas drawn from real-life applications.

Micro-Case Study: The Peeragogy Project, Year 2

10 new handbook contributors joined in the project's second year. We've begun a series of weekly Hangouts on Air that have brought in many additional discussants, all key people who can help to fulfil peeragogy's promise. The handbook has been considerably improved through edits and discussion. The next step for us is putting this work into action in the *Peeragogy Accelerator*.

CHAPTER 34

RECOMMENDED READING

Which is more fun, skateboarding or physics?
On the subject of fun and boredom

1. Kano, J. (1995/2013). THE CONTRIBUTION OF JUDO TO EDUCATION by Jigoro Kano.

2. Pale King, unfinished novel, by David Foster Wallace

3. On the Poverty of Student Life, by Mustapha Khayati

How do we know if we've won?

1. Forming, Norming, Storming, Performing (from Bruce Tuckman)

2. The "five-stage e-moderating model" (from Gilly Salmon)

3. I, We, Its, It (from Ken Wilber — for an application in modeling educational systems, see [1])

4. Assimilative, Information Processing, Communicative, Productive, Experiential, Adaptive (from Martin Oliver and Gráinne Conole)

5. Guidance & Support, Communication & Collaboration, Reflection & Demonstration, Content & Activities (from Gráinne Conole)

6. Considered in terms of "Learning Power" (Ruth Deakin-Crick *et al.*)

7. Multiple intelligences (after Howard Gardner)

8. The associated "mental state" (after Mihaly Csíkszentmihályi; see picture)

Motivation

1. Simon Sinek, Start With Why: How Great Leaders Inspire Everyone To Take Action, Penguin Books, 2011

Case Study: 5PH1NX

1. Senge, Peter. "The fifth discipline: The art and science of the learning organization." *New York: Currency Doubleday* (1990).

Patterns

Further readings on patterns

1. THE TIMELESS WAY OF BUILDING, by Christopher Alexander.

2. Article, "Manifesto 1991" by Christopher Alexander, Progressive Architecture, July 1991, pp. 108–112, provides a brief summary of Alexander's ideas in the form of a critique of mainstream architecture. Many of the same sorts of critical points would carry over to mainstream education. Some highlights are excerpted HERE.

3. WIKIPATTERNS

4. THE ORIGINS OF PATTERN THEORY, THE FUTURE OF THE THEORY, AND THE GENERATION OF A LIVING WORLD, Christopher Alexander's talk at the 1996 ACM Conference on Object-Oriented Programs, Systems, Languages and Applications (OOPSLA)

Other related work

1. CLUETRAIN MANIFESTO (the FIRST EDITION is available for free)

2. NEW RULES FOR THE NEW ECONOMY(YOU CAN ALSOREAD THE BOOK ONLINE)

3. OpenHatch.org, "an open source community aiming to help newcomers find their way into free software projects."

On Newcomers

1. Why do newcomers abandon open source software projects? (sildes by Igor Steinmacher and coauthors)

Antipatterns

1. Sapir-Whorf Hypothesis

2. Bourdieu's notion of "symbolic violence".

3. These fifteen properties are the glue which binds wholeness together - Christopher Alexander's more recent work, going beyond the idea of a pattern language.

Convening a Group

1. Engeström, Y. (1999). Innovative learning in work teams: Analyzing cycles of knowledge creation in practice. In Y. Engeström, R. Miettinen & R.-L-. Punamäki (Eds.), *Perspectives on activity theory*, (pp. 377-404). Cambridge, UK: Cambridge University Press

2. Gersick, C. (1988). Time and transition in work teams: Toward a new model of group development. *Academy of Management Journal* 31 (Oct.): 9-41.

3. Mimi Ito's observations about manga fan groups co-learning Japanese

4. Rheingold U, MindAmp groups

5. Shneiderman, B. (2007). Creativity support tools: accelerating discovery and innovation. *Commun. ACM* 50, 12 (December 2007), 20-32.

6. David de Ugarte, Phyles. (Summary) (Book)

7. Scheidel, T. M., & Crowell, L. (1964). Idea development in small discussion groups. *Quarterly Journal of Speech*, 50, 140-145.

8. Scheidel, T. M., & Crowell, L. (1979), *Discussing and Deciding - A Desk Book for Group Leaders and Members*, Macmillan Publishing

9. Ozturk and Simsek, "Of Conflict in Virtual Learning Communiities in the Context of a Democratic Pedagogy: A paradox or sophism?," in *Proceedings of the Networked Learning Conference, 2012, Maastricht.* VIDEO or TEXT.

10. Paragogy Handbook, How to Organize a MOOC

11. Cathy Davidson et al., How a Class Becomes a Community

K-12 Peeragogy

amazing technology tools for your classroom:

- Richard Byrne
- Sylvia Tolisano
- Caitlin Tucker
- Vicki Davis

How to develop your PLN:

- Degrees of Connected Teaching by Rodd Lucier
- TeachThought

Theory & philosophy of connnected learning for classroom transformation:

- David Truss

Recommended Reading

- STEVEN DOWNES
- WILL RICHARDSON

Adding Structure with Activities

1. THE D.SCHOOL BOOTCAMP BOOTLEG (CC-By-NC-SA) includes lots of fun activities to try. Can you crack the code and define new ones that are equally cool?
2. Puzio, R. S. (2005). "On free math and copyright bottlenecks." *Free Culture and the Digital Library Symposium Proceedings.*

Connectivism in Practice — How to Organize a MOOC (Massive Open Online Class)

1. Downes & Siemens MOOC SITE
2. WHAT CONNECTIVISM IS by Stephen Downes
3. AN INTRODUCTION TO CONNECTIVE KNOWLEDGE by Stephen Downes
4. FACILITATING A MASSIVE OPEN ONLINE COURSE, by Stephen Downes
5. GRSSHOPPER
6. CONNECTIVISM: A LEARNING THEORY FOR THE DIGITAL AGE by George Siemens
7. A CONNECTIVISM GLOSSARY
8. RHIZOMES AND NETWORKS by George Siemens
9. RHIZOMATIC EDUCATION: COMMUNITY AS CURRICULUM by Dave Cormier
10. KNOWING KNOWLEDGE, a book by George Siemens

11. NET SMART, Howard Rheingold (about internal and external literacies for coping with the 'always on' digital era)

12. MASSIVE OPEN ONLINE COURSES: Setting Up (StartTo-MOOC, Part 1)

13. THE MOOC GUIDE

Co-Facilitation

1. PEER EDUCATION: TRAINING OF TRAINERS MANUAL; UN Interagency Group on Young Peoples Health

2. CO FACILITATING: Advantages & Potential Disadvantages. J. Willam Pfeifer and John E Johnes

3. SUMMARY of John Heron's model of the role of facilitators

4. CARL ROGERS, CORE CONDITIONS AND EDUCATION, Encyclopedia of Informal Education

5. PEER MEDIATION, Study Guides and Strategies

6. CO-FACILITATION: THE ADVANTAGES AND CHALLENGES, Canadian Union of Public Employees

7. BOHEMIA INTERACTIVE COMMUNITY WIKI GUIDELINES

8. Barrett-Lennard, G. T. (1998) CARL ROGER'S HELPING SYSTEM. JOURNEY AND SUBSTANCE, London: Sage

9. 5 PILLARS OF WIKIPEDIA, from Wikipedia

10. TRAINING THE FORCE (2002) US Army Field Manual #FM 7-0 (FM 25-100)

11. LEARNING REIMAGINED: PARTICIPATORY, PEER, GLOBAL, ONLINE, by Howard Rheingold

12. RESEARCH GATE is a network dedicated to science and research, in which members connect, collaborate and discover scientific publications, jobs and conferences.

13. CREATING AND FACILITATING PEER SUPPORT GROUPS, by The Community Tool Box

14. FACILITATION TIPS, by Villanova University

15. HERDING PASSIONATE CATS: THE ROLE OF FACILITATOR IN A PEER LEARNING, by Pippa Buchanan

16. REFLECTIVE PEER FACILITATION: CRAFTING COLLABORATIVE SELF-ASSESSMENT, by Dale Vidmar, Southern Oregon University Library

17. EFFECTIVE CO-FACILITATION, by Everywoman's Center, University of Massachussetts

18. "TEACHING SMART PEOPLE HOW TO LEARN" by Chris Argyris, Harvard Business Review 69.3, 1991; also published in expanded form as a BOOK with the same name.

Assessment

1. Morgan, C. and M. O'Reilly. (1999). ASSESSING OPEN AND DISTANCE LEARNERS. London: Kogan Page Limited.

2. Schmidt, J. P., Geith, C., Håklev, S. and J. Thierstein. (2009). PEER-TO-PEER RECOGNITION OF LEARNING IN OPEN EDUCATION. *International Review of Research in Open and Distance Learning.* Volume 10, Number 5.

3. L.S. Vygotsky: MIND IN SOCIETY: DEVELOPMENT OF HIGHER PSYCHOLOGICAL PROCESSES

4. REIJO MIETTINEN and JAAKKO VIRKKUNEN, EPISTEMIC OBJECTS, ARTIFACTS AND ORGANIZATIONAL CHANGE, *Organization*, May 2005, 12: 437-456.

Technologies, Services, and Platforms

1. Irene Greif and Sunil Sarin (1987): Data Sharing in Group Work, ACM Transactions on Office Information Systems, vol. 5, no. 2, April 1987, pp. 187-211.

2. Irene Greif (ed.) (1988): Computer-Supported Cooperative Work: A Book of Readings, San Mateo, CA: Morgan Kaufman.

3. Irene Greif (1988): Remarks in panel discussion on "CSCW: What does it mean?", CSCW '88. Proceedings of the Conference on Computer-Supported Cooperative Work, September 26-28, 1988, Portland, Oregon, ACM, New York, NY.

4. Kamnersgaard, 1988

5. Vessey & Galletta, 1991

6. Norman, 2001, 2003

7. DeSanctis & Pool, 2004

Real-Time Meetings

1. Howard Rheingold's webconferencing BOOKMARKS

Additional Tips from an open source perspective

Care of User:Neophyte on the Teaching Open Source wiki.

1. The Art of Community

2. Open Advice

3. The Open Source Way

Recommended Reading

Forums

1. Rheingold, H. WHY USE FORUMS? *Social Media Classroom.*

2. Rheingold, H. (1998). THE ART OF HOSTING GOOD CONVERSATIONS ONLINE.

3. Gallagher, E. J. (2006). GUIDELINES FOR DISCUSSION BOARD WRITING. Lehigh University.

4. Gallagher, E.J. (2009). SHAPING A CULTURE OF CONVERSATION. THE DISCUSSION BOARD AND BEYOND. The Academic Commons.

5. Academic Technology Center. (2010). IMPROVING THE USE OF DISCUSSION BOARDS. Worcester Polytechnic Institute.

Still more recommended reading

On Paragogy

1. Corneli, J. (2010). IMPLEMENTING PARAGOGY. Lesson plan.

2. Corneli, J. and C. Danoff. (2010/2013). *Paragogy.* paragogy.net

On Learning vs Training

1. Hart, J. (April 20th, 2012). IS IT TIME FOR A BYOL (BRING YOUR OWN LEARNING) STRATEGY FOR YOUR ORGANIZATION? *Learning in the Social Space. Jane Hart's Blog.*

On PLNs

1. Rheingold, H. (2010). SHELLY TERRELL: GLOBAL NETWEAVER, CURATOR, PLN BUILDER. *DML Central.*

2. Richardson, W. and R. Mancabelli. (2011). PERSONAL LEARNING NETWORKS: USING THE POWER OF CONNECTION TO TRANSFORM EDUCATION. Bloomington, IN: Solution Tree Press.

3. Howard Rheingold's PLN links on Delicious

A word list for your inner edu-geek

You can read about all of these things on Wikipedia.

1. CONSTRUCTIVISM
2. SOCIAL CONSTRUCTIVISM
3. RADICAL CONSTRUCTIVISM
4. ENACTIVISM
5. CONSTRUCTIONISM
6. CONNECTIVISM

CHAPTER 35

STYLE GUIDE

This is a How-To Handbook.

Keep it short. The easiest sections to read are those that are shorter and include some kind of visual (video or image) and have some personal connection (i.e. they tell a story). For anything longer, break it up into sub-pages, add visuals, make sure each sub-page is accessible to someone (who is it?). Think clearly of this reader, talk to them.

Make it clear. We'll illustrate this point by example. The original full title of the book was "The Peeragogy Handbook: A resource for self-organizing self-learners". But "SELF-ORGANIZING" is a technical term, and "self-learner" is a confusing neologism. We shouldn't use technical terms unless we explain them. So we really shouldn't use it in the first sentence or paragraph, or title, of the book because we'll scare people off or confuse them. If we want to explain what "self-organization" means and why it is relevant for peeragogy, then we can take a chapter to do that much later on in the book. At the same time, we shouldn't try to "say the same thing in a simpler way." We should try to get rid of the technical concept completely and see what's left. The easiest thing to do in such cases is to delete the sentence completely and start over: when in doubt, speak plainly.

Don't overdo it with bullet points. Text can be very hard to read when there are more than a few bullet points included. Numbered lists should also be used sparingly. It also seems that when many disjointed bullet points appear, sometimes the author is really just indexing the main points that are presented better in someone else's narrative. Therefor, consider replacing an entire bulleted list with a reference to someone else's book/webpage/chapter. In today's hyperlinked world, it's easy enough for the reader to go elsewhere to get good content (and indeed, we should make it easy for them to find the best treatments around!). It is not very pleasant to have to *read* a taxonomy.

Include activities. When reading, editing or otherwise working your way through the book, please make note of any activities or exercises that come to mind, and share them. We're always striving to be more practical and applicable.

Don't be overly chatty. In our efforts to escape from academia-speak and simplify the text in the handbook, it's important to make sure we are not heading towards the other extreme – being too conversational. When we're having a conversation with someone, we tend to pepper our ideas with transitional or pivotal phrases ("In any event," "With that said," "As I mentioned elsewhere," etc.) that help to keep the talk flowing. We also go off on brief tangents before making our way back to the main topic, and sometimes express ourselves in run-on sentences. While this is perfectly natural in speech, it can be confusing and complex in written text. Let's strive for the perfect balance of simple yet professional writing.

Additional style bonus points

- Avoid double lines after paragraphs; this is a leftover from the age of typewriters and can create "rivers" of white space.

- Capitalize the first word of each item in a bulleted list, especially if items include a verb form (this list is an example!). Punctuate uniformly.

- Capitalize the first word of headings and subheadings; lower case all others.

Style Guide

Format your HTML nicely. We need to be able to process the content from this Wordpress site and turn it into various formats like LaTeX and EPUB. Our automated tools work much better if pages are formatted with simple and uniform HTML markup. Some key points:

- Mark up your links: use The Peeragogy Handbook instead of http://peeragogy.org. It's best if the link text is somewhat descriptive.

- Use a numbered list to format your references (see Convening a Group for one example of an article that gets this right!)

- Use Heading 2 and Heading 3 tags to mark up sections, not **bold** text. If you use bold or italics in your paragraphs, you should **check** that the markup *is actually correct*. It should exactly surround the words that you're marking up – `<em>like this</em>` – and it should not include extra spaces around marked up words – `<em> NOT like this </em>`.

- Be aware that Wordpress does not always add paragraph tags to your paragraphs.

- Wordpress also tries to replace straight quote marks with "smart quotes", but it sometimes doesn't achieve the aim. If you notice weird quotemarks (especially in the PDF version), you can add smart quote marks by hand.

CHAPTER 36

MEET THE AUTHORS

Bryan Alexander — USA, VT (Author) I research the ways new technologies change education, teaching, learning, and scholarship. I'm passionate about storytelling, gaming, pedagogy, and understanding the future. My family homesteads on top of a little mountain, raising food.

Paul Allison — USA, NY (Author) Currently, I teach English at the BRONX ACADEMY SENIOR HIGH. Another community that I'm a part of is the NEW YORK CITY WRITING PROJECT. I'm the NYC Technology Liaison for the NATIONAL WRITING PROJECT. I help to manage YOUTH VOICES and I co-produce TEACHERS TEACHING TEACHERS.

María F. Arenas — República Argentina (Author, Editor) Independent consultant researcher on TICS applied to Learning, Digital Communication, Institutional, Corporate. On line facilitator tutorship. Professor on Semiotics, Social Communication, Networking.

Régis Barondeau — Canada (Author) I build bridges between research, praxeology and technology and I become creative "by finding a likeness between things which were not thought alike before" (Bronowski, 1958). I'm interested in complexity, culture, social media especially wikis, education, open government and more.

Doug Breitbart — USA, NJ (Author, Meeting Support) I a catalyst and provocateur who has worn the hats of attorney, consultant, facilitator, coach, entrepreneur, father, husband, student, teacher.

Meet the Authors

George Brett — USA, VA (Author, Edior, Meeting Support) Twitter Bio: "autodidactic techno arsty craftsy eclecticist." Many years as a diplomat for IT technology as applied to research and education. I'm a teacher/trainer, consultant, analyst, info ferret, artist, lifelong learner, and member of a great family. Current challenges include: best way to share skills and experiences with others and as a Gen-Boomer finding more steady work.

Suz Burroughs - USA, CA (Author, Designer) I enable the connections between the teacher and learner in all of us by designing robust, measurable learning environments where people share their knowledge and experience with each other. Learning Designer, Design Thinking facilitator, Visiting Professor of Innovation.

Joe Corneli — U.K. (Author, Editor) Joe Corneli does research on the anthropology of modern mathematics. He is a member of the board of directors of the US-based nonprofit, PlanetMath.org, and a research student at the Knowledge Media Institute of The Open University, UK.

Jay Cross — USA, CA (Author) Jay is the Johnny Appleseed of informal learning. The INTERNET TIME ALLIANCE, which he chairs, helps corporations and governments use networks to accelerate performance.

Charles Jeffrey Danoff — USA, IL (Author) Charles is the Owner of Mr. Danoff's Teaching Laboratory, an Educational Publishing and Services firm he established in 2009. He started co-publishing research on Paragogy, Peeragogy's inspiration, in late 2010.

James Folkestad - USA, CO (Author, Editor, Designer, Developer) My approach to education has shifted from an emphasis on my teaching, to a more central focus on student learning, and finally to an activity-systems approach as I have come to realize that the two (teacher and learner) are inseparable parts of the learning ecosystem.

Meet the Authors

John Graves - Australia (Editor) Founder of SlideSpeech. Graduate of Singularity University.

Gigi Johnson, EdD — USA, CA (Author, Developer) I mix formal learning programs with programs to help learners begin to work, live, and create everywhere. My own adventures include writing, singing, video, teaching, and parenting 3 teens.

Anna Keune — Germany/Finland (Co-author, Designer) I design technology for learning and I like it. I'm affiliated with the Media Lab Helsinki, Aalto University School of Arts, Design and Architecture.

Meet the Authors

Kyle Larson — FL, USA (Editor) Kyle Larson is an undergraduate thesis student at New College of Florida. His research interests include composition theory, rhetorical theory, computers and composition, and pedagogy.

Roland Legrand — Belgium (Author) I'm a financial journalist, heavily involved in experimenting with social media and new forms for reporting and community conversation.

Amanda Lyons — USA, NY Designer I am a Visual Practitioner, Organization Development Consultant & Experiential Educator. I love helping people communicate via visual tools that generally include markers and paper. I think our education system could benefit from using visual communication tools as well as text based methods.

Meet the Authors

Christopher Neal — USA, WA (Communications and Media) I am driven by technology and its ability to modify virtual communities and social media, and a passion for Social:Learn, Social:iA, Situated Cognition, Social Learning Theory, Connectivism, etc.

Ted Newcomb — USA, AZ (Author, Project Management) Happily retired grandpa, curating on digital culture, sociology of the web; interested in collaboration and cooperation in digital networks that result in positive change.

Charlotte Pierce — USA, MA (Editor, Publisher) Indie publisher who finds happiness in pushing her limits and seeing them back down. Augmented her intellect in RheingoldU's Think-Know Tools course, then joined the amazing Peeragogy community, where the plot thickens.

Howard Rheingold — USA, CA (Author, Editor) Inspired by Charles Danoff and Joe Corneli's work on paragogy, I instigated the Peeragogy project in order to provide a resource for self-organizing self-learners. Learning is my passion.

Paola Ricaurte — Mexico (Author) My believe: education and technology are essential tools for social change. My challenges: activist, teacher, mother, immigrant. My philosophy: I am what I am because of who we all are.

Fabrizio Terzi — Italy (Inventor, Designer, Translator) I am involved in social and educational projects related to public access to knowledge and cultural diversity. I am an active member of FSF and the FTG – working on Free Culture.

Meet the Authors

Geoff Walker — U.K. (Author) A Further and Higher Education Lecturer and Tutor, social networker, e-learning advocate.

CHAPTER 37

WEB PAGES CITED IN THIS BOOK

p. 1
    I told the story of how I've used social media in teaching and learning...
        HTTP://VIMEO.COM/35685124

p. 2
    wiki...
        HTTP://SOCIALMEDIACLASSROOM.COM/HOST/PEERAGOGY/

p. 9
    Wikipedia article...
        HTTPS://EN.WIKIPEDIA.ORG/WIKI/PEER_LEARNING
    search on YouTube...
        HTTP://WWW.YOUTUBE.COM/RESULTS?SEARCH_QUERY=
        PEERAGOGY&SM=3
    G+ community...
        HTTPS://PLUS.GOOGLE.COM/COMMUNITIES/
        107386162349686249470

p. 24
    Platon Cave Sanraedam (1604)...
        HTTP://COMMONS.WIKIMEDIA.ORG/W/INDEX.PHP?TITLE=FILE:
        PLATON_CAVE_SANRAEDAM_1604.JPG&OLDID=68567627

p. 25
    StoryCorps...
        HTTP://STORYCORPS.ORG/ABOUT/

p. 39
    Challenge vs. Skill...
        HTTP://COMMONS.WIKIMEDIA.ORG/WIKI/FILE%3ACHALLENGE_
        VS_SKILL.SVG

p. 46
    Next Door Cafe...
        HTTPS://WWW.NEXTDOORCHI.COM/

p. 47
    Peeragogy Accelerator...
        HTTP://COMMONSABUNDANCE.NET/DOCS/HELP-BUILD-THE-
        PEERAGOGY-ACCELERATOR-WORK-IN-PROGRESS/
    Cooperation in a Peer Production Economy: Experimental Evidence from Wikipedia...
        HTTPS://CYBER.LAW.HARVARD.EDU/INTERACTIVE/EVENTS/
        LUNCHEONS/2013/11/JEROME

p. 52

Laughing Heart...
> HTTP://WWW.YOUTUBE.COM/WATCH?V=BHOHI5UEO0A

p. 54
Capture the event on video & post it to your blog....
> HTTP://ALARHSENGLITCOMP.BLOGSPOT.COM/2012/12/FEATS-OF-WISDOM-1_15.HTML

p. 57
Future of Work Report 2013...
> HTTP://WWW.SLIDESHARE.NET/PSFK/PSFK-PRESENTS-FUTURE-OF-WORK-REPORT

p. 69
m...
> HTTP://WEB.MEDIA.MIT.EDU/~MINSKY/OLPC-1.HTML

e...
> HTTP://WEB.MEDIA.MIT.EDU/~MINSKY/OLPC-2.HTML

m...
> HTTP://WEB.MEDIA.MIT.EDU/~MINSKY/OLPC-3.HTML

o...
> HTTP://WEB.MEDIA.MIT.EDU/~MINSKY/OLPC-4.HTML

s...
> HTTP://WEB.MEDIA.MIT.EDU/~MINSKY/OLPC-5.HTML

p. 71
Patterns of Software...
> HTTP://DREAMSONGS.NET/FILES/PATTERNSOFSOFTWARE.PDF

p. 73
suggested...
> HTTP://SOCIALMEDIACLASSROOM.COM/HOST/PEERAGOGY/WIKI/ROLESDIVISION-LABOR

wiki page...
> HTTP://SOCIALMEDIACLASSROOM.COM/HOST/PEERAGOGY/

p. 75
knowledge cartography...
> HTTP://KNOWLEDGECARTOGRAPHY.ORG/

meaning making...
> HTTP://WWW.HITL.WASHINGTON.EDU/PUBLICATIONS/R-97-47/TWO.HTML

p. 77
examples...
> HTTP://CAMPUS.FTACADEMY.ORG/WIKI/INDEX.PHP/FREE_TECHNOLOGY_GUILD#LEARNING_DESIGN

Independent Publishers of New England...
> HTTP://IPNE.ORG

p. 80

progressive stack...
: http://en.wikipedia.org/wiki/Progressive_stack
Nick Haus...
: http://www.nickhaus.com/2010/02/afternoon-remembered-complete-with.html

p. 83
Quoted by Andrew Murphy...
: http://nine.fibreculturejournal.org/

p. 85
Misunderstanding Power (Laws)...
: http://socialmediaclassroom.com/host/peeragogy/forum/anti-patterns-concerns-complaints-and-critiques#comment-1854

p. 86
Massively Distributed Authorship of Academic Papers...
: http://altchi.org/submissions/submission_wmt_0.pdf
size of cities...
: http://www2.econ.uu.nl/users/marrewijk/geography/zipf/index.htm
energy use...
: http://pricetags.wordpress.com/2010/10/26/kleibers-law-growth-and-creativity-in-cities/

p. 87
The Uncertainty Principle, Volume II, Issue 3...
: http://www.theuncertaintyprinciple.danoff.org/v2i3.html
Zipf's law...
: http://en.wikipedia.org/w/index.php?title=Zipf%27s_law&oldid=575709945
Beating the averages...
: http://www.paulgraham.com/avg.html

p. 88
double bind...
: http://en.wikipedia.org/wiki/Double_bind
Isolation...
: http://socialmediaclassroom.com/host/peeragogy/forum/anti-patterns-concerns-complaints-and-critiques#comment-2267
Navel-Gazing...
: http://socialmediaclassroom.com/host/peeragogy/forum/anti-patterns-concerns-complaints-and-critiques#comment-1808

p. 89
Carrying Capacity...

>   HTTP://SOCIALMEDIACLASSROOM.COM/HOST/PEERAGOGY/
>   FORUM/PATTERNS-AND-USE-CASES#COMMENT-2320

p. 90

> Facebook and the Strength of Weak Ties...
>   HTTP://WWW.PSYCHOLOGYTODAY.COM/BLOG/THINKING-ABOUT-
>   KIDS/201005/FACEBOOK-AND-THE-STRENGTH-WEAK-TIES

p. 91

> Kevin Slavin's TED talk...
>   HTTP://WWW.TED.COM/TALKS/KEVIN_SLAVIN_HOW_
>   ALGORITHMS_SHAPE_OUR_WORLD.HTML
>
> All our grievances are interconnected...
>   HTTP://WWW.NYCGA.NET/FILES/2011/11/
>   DECLARATIONFLOWCHART_V2_LARGE.JPG

p. 92

> Multiple PSK31 transmissions on the 20m digital modes band at around 14.07 MHz...
>   HTTPS://COMMONS.WIKIMEDIA.ORG/WIKI/FILE:PSK_MATRIX.
>   JPG

p. 95

> A. T. Ariyaratne...
>   HTTP://WWW.SARVODAYAUSA.ORG/LEARN/A-T-ARIYARTNE/
> collected works...
>   HTTP://WWW.SARVODAYA.ORG/ABOUT/PHILOSOPHY/COLLECTED-
>   WORKS-VOL-1/RURAL-SELF-HELP

p. 96

> Simon Sinek...
>   HTTP://EN.WIKIPEDIA.ORG/WIKI/SIMON_SINEK

p. 100

> Tuckman-like outline...
>   HTTP://EN.WIKIPEDIA.ORG/WIKI/FORMING-STORMING-
>   NORMING-PERFORMING

p. 101

> Of Conflict in Virtual Learning Communiities in the Context of a Democratic Pedagogy: A paradox or sophism?...
>   HTTP://NETWORKEDLEARNINGCONFERENCE.ORG.UK/ABSTRACTS/
>   PDF/OZTURK.PDF

p. 105

> Go...
>   HTTP://SENSEIS.XMP.NET/?MYTHOFORIGIN
> Chess...
>   HTTP://WWW.AMAZON.COM/CHESS-SUCCESS-USING-STRENGTHS-
>   CHILDREN/DP/0767915682
> Oblique Strategies...
>   HTTP://WWW.RTQE.NET/OBLIQUESTRATEGIES/

Clip Kino...
: HTTP://CLIPKINO.INFO/

p. 107
observes...
: HTTP://WWW.HUFFINGTONPOST.COM/STEPHEN-DOWNES/THE-ROLE-OF-THE-EDUCATOR_B_790937.HTML

Connected Educator's Starter Kit...
: HTTPS://DL.DROPBOXUSERCONTENT.COM/U/38904447/STARTER-KIT-FINAL.PDF

p. 108
'follow' other users on Twitter...
: HTTP://WWW.FRACTUSLEARNING.COM/2012/05/25/TWITTER-FOLLOW-EDUCATION-TECHNOLOGY/

educational Twitter 'chats'...
: HTTP://CYBRARYMAN.COM/CHATS.HTML

blogs...
: HTTP://THEINNOVATIVEEDUCATOR.BLOGSPOT.CA/2012/04/TEN-BEST-EDUCATION-BLOGS.HTML

Facebook...
: HTTP://WWW.EDSOCIALMEDIA.COM/2011/02/THE-ADVANTAGE-OF-FACEBOOK-GROUPS-IN-EDUCATION/

Edmodo...
: HTTP://WWW.SLIDESHARE.NET/CMSDSQUIRES/EDMODO-FOR-TEACHERS-GUIDE

LinkedIn...
: HTTP://WWW.EMERGINGEDTECH.COM/2012/02/8-GREAT-LINKEDIN-GROUPS-FOR-EDUCATORS/

blog...
: HTTP://EDUDEMIC.COM/2012/08/EDUCATION-BLOGS/?UTM_MEDIUM=TWITTER&UTM_SOURCE=TWITTERFEED

wiki...
: HTTP://EDUCATIONALWIKIS.WIKISPACES.COM/EXAMPLES+OF+EDUCATIONAL+WIKIS

Classroom 2.0...
: HTTP://WWW.CLASSROOM20.COM/

Steve Hargadon....
: HTTP://WWW.STEVEHARGADON.COM/

Blackboard Collaborate...
: HTTP://WWW.FUTUREOFEDUCATION.COM/PAGE/PAST-INTERVIEWS

p. 109
strategies...
: HTTP://STORIFY.COM/DIGIPHILE/HOW-TO-BUILD-A-PERSONAL-LEARNING-NETWORK-ON-TWITTE

Connected Learning TV...
: http://connectedlearning.tv/howard-rheingold-social-media-and-peer-learning-mediated-pedagogy-peeragogy

TechTalkTuesdays...
: http://techtalktuesdays.global2.vic.edu.au/

VolunteersNeeded...
: http://learning2gether.pbworks.com/w/page/32206114/volunteersneeded

SimpleK12...
: http://simplek12.com/webinars

K12 Online,...
: http://k12onlineconference.org/

CEET...
: http://www.learnnowbc.ca/educators/moodlemeets/default.aspx

EdTechTalk...
: http://edtechtalk.com/taxonomy/term/130

P2PU's...
: https://p2pu.org/en/schools/school-of-ed-pilot/

TeachThought...
: http://www.teachthought.com/

PD On Demand...
: http://www.livebinders.com/play/play_or_edit?id=429095

EduCon...
: http://educonphilly.org/

EdCamps...
: http://davidwees.com/content/what-edcamp

THATcamp...
: http://thatcamp.org/

ConnectedCA...
: http://connectedcanada.org/

p. 110

infographic...
: http://farm9.staticflickr.com/8160/7161689001_9b6725a4ca_h.jpg

p. 111

Self-Organizing Learning Environment...
: http://en.wikipedia.org/wiki/Self_Organised_Learning_Environment

p. 112

A visualization of the facilitated peer to peer SOLE (http://goo.gl/7StkJK)...
: http://goo.gl/7StkJK

p. 113

Sugata Mitra...
: http://sugatam.wikispaces.com/
SOLE Tool Kit...
: http://www.ted.com/pages/sole_toolkit
Universal Design for Learning...
: http://www.udlcenter.org/aboutudl/udlguidelines
hole in the wall...
: http://www.ted.com/talks/sugata_mitra_shows_how_kids_teach_themselves.html

p. 114

learning a game...
: http://www.academia.edu/1137269/Game-based_Learning_and_Intrinsic_Motivation
hidden curriculum...
: http://en.wikipedia.org/wiki/Hidden_curriculum
transformed learning environment...
: http://www.scribd.com/doc/181089012/Transformed-Learning-Environment-Analysis
overwhelming influence, on learning...
: http://scholar.lib.vt.edu/theses/available/etd-09232007-220306/unrestricted/SElmasryETDbodytext.pdf
loosely connected adaptive complex systems...
: http://nourdiab.wordpress.com/2011/02/23/the-theories-of-christopher-alexander/

p. 115

Universally Designed Context...
: http://www.cast.org/library/UDLguidelines/
learner generated syllabus [...
: http://www.theatreprof.com/2011/active-learning-student-generated-syllabus/
user generated education...
: http://usergeneratededucation.wordpress.com/
just-in-time learning...
: http://www.wordstream.com/blog/ws/2013/10/02/just-in-time-information-hacks
dichroic...
: http://en.wikipedia.org/wiki/Dichroic_filter

p. 119

Facebook as a Supplemental LMS...
: http://community.telecentre.org/profiles/blogs/facebook-as-a-supplemental-lms
Reciprocal Apprenticeships...
: http://starwars.wikia.com/wiki/Reciprocal_Apprenticeship

About Sugata Mitra...
   http://sugatam.wikispaces.com/
The SOLE Toolkit...
   http://www.ted.com/pages/sole_toolkit
Universal Design for Learning Guidelines...
   http://www.udlcenter.org/aboutudl/udlguidelines
The child-driven education...
   http://www.ted.com/talks/sugata_mitra_the_child_driven_education.html
Game-based Learning and Intrinsic Motivation by Kristi Mead...
   http://www.academia.edu/1137269/Game-based_Learning_and_Intrinsic_Motivation
Hidden Curriculum...
   http://en.wikipedia.org/wiki/Hidden_curriculum

p. 120

Transformed Learning Environment Analysis...
   http://www.scribd.com/doc/181089012/Transformed-Learning-Environment-Analysis
Integration Patterns of Learning Technologies...
   http://scholar.lib.vt.edu/theses/available/etd-09232007-220306/unrestricted/SElmasryETDbodytext.pdf
In-Forming singular/plural design, The Theories of Christopher Alexander...
   http://nourdiab.wordpress.com/2011/02/23/the-theories-of-christopher-alexander/
Overwhelmed with Blog Tips? Hack Learning with Just In Time Information...
   http://www.wordstream.com/blog/ws/2013/10/02/just-in-time-information-hacks
Dichroic Filter...
   http://en.wikipedia.org/wiki/Dichroic_filter
UDL Guidelines...
   http://www.cast.org/library/UDLguidelines/
Active Learning Student Generated Syllabus...
   http://www.theatreprof.com/2011/active-learning-student-generated-syllabus/
User Generated Education Blog...
   http://usergeneratededucation.wordpress.com/
Facebook as a Supplemental LMS...
   http://community.telecentre.org/profiles/blogs/facebook-as-a-supplemental-lms
Reciprocal Apprenticeship...
   http://starwars.wikia.com/wiki/Reciprocal_Apprenticeship

p. 126
> our paper...
>> HTTP://PARAGOGY.NET/PARAGOGYPAPER2

p. 127
> Open Knowledge Conference (OKCon)...
>> HTTP://OKFN.ORG/OKCON/
>
> paragogy.net...
>> HTTP://PARAGOGY.NET

p. 133
> 'Peer learning' as pedagogic discourse for research education...
>> HTTP://MANAINKBLOG.TYPEPAD.COM/FAULTLINES/FILES/BOUDLEE2005.PDF
>
> Paragogy...
>> HTTP://CEUR-WS.ORG/VOL-739/PAPER_5.PDF
>
> Personalised and Peer-Supported Learning: The Peer-to-Peer Learning Environment (P2PLE)...
>> HTTP://GREAV.UB.EDU/DER/INDEX.PHP/DER/ARTICLE/VIEW/188/330
>
> Paragogical Praxis...
>> HTTP://PARAGOGY.NET/PARAGOGICALPRAXISPAPER

p. 136
> Zed Shaw's task-management trick...
>> HTTP://LEARNPYTHONTHEHARDWAY.ORG/BOOK/INTRO.HTML#COMMENT-409972596

p. 139
> KS ToolKit...
>> HTTP://WWW.KSTOOLKIT.ORG/KS+METHODS
>
> Designing Effective and Innovative Sources...
>> HTTP://SERC.CARLETON.EDU/NAGTWORKSHOPS/COURSEDESIGN/TUTORIAL/STRATEGIES.HTML

p. 145
> questions that require storytelling...
>> HTTP://EN.WIKIPEDIA.ORG/WIKI/CRITICAL_INCIDENT_TECHNIQUE
>
> superlative...
>> HTTP://EN.WIKIPEDIA.ORG/WIKI/SUPERLATIVE
>
> close-ended questions...
>> HTTP://EN.WIKIPEDIA.ORG/WIKI/CLOSED-ENDED_QUESTION
>
> Connectivist...
>> HTTP://WWW.ELEARNSPACE.ORG/ARTICLES/CONNECTIVISM.HTM

p. 146
> netiquette...
>> HTTP://EN.WIKIPEDIA.ORG/WIKI/NETIQUETTE#NETIQUETTE
>
> flaming...

>   HTTP://EN.WIKIPEDIA.ORG/WIKI/FLAMING_%28INTERNET%29
>
> shared calendar...
>> HTTP://SUPPORT.GOOGLE.COM/CALENDAR/BIN/ANSWER.PY?HL=
>> EN&ANSWER=36598

p. 147

> shared document...
>> HTTPS://SUPPORT.GOOGLE.COM/DRIVE/BIN/ANSWER.PY?HL=
>> EN&ANSWER=143213&TOPIC=21010&CTX=TOPIC
>
> spreadsheet...
>> HTTPS://SUPPORT.GOOGLE.COM/DRIVE/BIN/ANSWER.PY?HL=
>> EN&ANSWER=141195&TOPIC=20329&CTX=TOPIC
>
> form...
>> HTTP://SUPPORT.GOOGLE.COM/DRIVE/BIN/ANSWER.PY?HL=
>> EN&ANSWER=87809

p. 151

> Coursera...
>> HTTPS://WWW.COURSERA.ORG/
>
> edX...
>> HTTPS://WWW.EDX.ORG/
>
> Udacity...
>> HTTP://WWW.UDACITY.COM/
>
> E-learning and Digital Cultures...
>> HTTPS://WWW.COURSERA.ORG/COURSE/EDC

p. 152

> categories of learning theories...
>> HTTP://RYAN2POINT0.WORDPRESS.COM/2010/01/12/TAXONOMY-
>> OF-LEARNING-THEORIES/
>
> connectivism...
>> HTTP://EN.WIKIPEDIA.ORG/WIKI/CONNECTIVISM
>
> disputed...
>> HTTP://EN.WIKIPEDIA.ORG/WIKI/TALK:CONNECTIVISM

p. 153

> Change11...
>> HTTP://CHANGE.MOOC.CA/ABOUT.HTM
>
> change.mooc.ca...
>> HTTP://CHANGE.MOOC.CA/INDEX.HTML
>
> how it works...
>> HTTP://CHANGE.MOOC.CA/HOW.HTM

p. 155

> Daily Newsletter...
>> HTTP://CHANGE.MOOC.CA/NEWSLETTER.HTM
>
> site...
>> HTTP://CHANGE.MOOC.CA/INDEX.HTML
>
> gRSShopper...

HTTP://GRSSHOPPER.DOWNES.CA/INDEX.HTML

p. 156

Add a New Feed...

HTTP://CHANGE.MOOC.CA/NEW_FEED.HTM

p. 157

Feed43...

HTTP://FEED43.COM

create an email news letter...

HTTP://WWW.WPBEGINNER.COM/WP-TUTORIALS/CREATE-A-FREE-EMAIL-NEWSLETTER-SERVICE-USING-WORDPRESS/%20

how to design and build an email newsletter without loosing your mind...

HTTP://WWW.SMASHINGMAGAZINE.COM/2010/01/19/DESIGN-AND-BUILD-AN-EMAIL-NEWSLETTER-WITHOUT-LOSING-YOUR-MIND/

p. 158

Facilitating a Massive Open Online Course...

HTTP://WWW.DOWNES.CA/PRESENTATION/290

How this Course Works...

HTTP://CHANGE.MOOC.CA/HOW.HTM

What is a MOOC...

HTTP://WWW.YOUTUBE.COM/WATCH?V=EW3GMGQCZQC

Success in a MOOC...

HTTP://WWW.YOUTUBE.COM/WATCH?V=R8AVYQ5ZQM0

Knowledge in a MOOC...

HTTP://WWW.YOUTUBE.COM/WATCH?V=BWKDHZSAAG0

Introduction and invitation...

HTTP://WWW.YOUTUBE.COM/WATCH?V=MQNYHLFNH3I

p. 167

http://cct.wikispaces.com/CEt...

HTTP://CCT.WIKISPACES.COM/CEt

http://cct.wikispaces.com/CEp...

HTTP://CCT.WIKISPACES.COM/CEp

http://bit.ly/etguide...

HTTP://BIT.LY/ETGUIDE

Supporting change in creative learning...

HTTP://WP.ME/P1GWFA-VV

p. 172

The Community Tool Box...

HTTP://CTB.KU.EDU/EN/TABLECONTENTS/SECTION_1180.ASPX

p. 173

Learning Re-imagined: Participatory, Peer, Global, Online...

HTTP://DMLCENTRAL.NET/BLOG/HOWARD-RHEINGOLD/LEARNING-REIMAGINED-PARTICIPATORY-PEER-GLOBAL-ONLINE

p. 180

Neutral Point of View...
    HTTP://EN.WIKIPEDIA.ORG/WIKI/WIKIPEDIA:NEUTRAL_POINT_OF_VIEW

p. 181
Project Management Body of Knowledge...
    HTTP://WWW.PMI.ORG/PMBOK-GUIDE-AND-STANDARDS.ASPX
Program Evaluation and Review Technic...
    HTTP://EN.WIKIPEDIA.ORG/WIKI/PERT
Gantt chart...
    HTTP://EN.WIKIPEDIA.ORG/WIKI/GANTT_CHART
90/9/1 rule...
    HTTP://EN.WIKIPEDIA.ORG/WIKI/1%25_RULE_%28INTERNET_CULTURE%29

p. 184
as many as...
    HTTP://%20HTTP://WWW.READWRITEWEB.COM/ARCHIVES/WIKIPEDIAS_GOAL_1_BILLION_MONTHLY_VISITORS_BY_2015.PHP
empirical fact...
    HTTP://WWW.AARONSW.COM/WEBLOG/WHOWRITESWIKIPEDIA

p. 185
mathematical fact...
    HTTP://EN.WIKIPEDIA.ORG/WIKI/N-SPHERE#VOLUME_AND_SURFACE_AREA
notoriety...
    HTTP://WWW.WIRED.COM/THREATLEVEL/2011/07/SWARTZ-ARREST/

p. 186
Coase's Penguin...
    HTTP://WWW.YALE.EDU/YALELJ/112/BENKLERWEB.PDF
quoting...
    HTTP://WWW.AARONSW.COM/WEBLOG/PERFECTINSTITUTIONS
PlanetMath...
    PLANETMATH.ORG

p. 189
5 rules for the evolution of cooperation...
    HTTP://ISITES.HARVARD.EDU/FS/DOCS/ICB.TOPIC426436.FILES/FIVE_RULES.PDF

p. 191
Peer Produced Peer Learning: A Mathematics Case Study...
    HTTP://METAMESO.ORG/~JOE/THESIS-OUTLINE.HTML
Five rules for the evolution of cooperation...
    HTTP://WWW.SCIENCEMAG.ORG/CONTENT/314/5805/1560.FULL

p. 197

Effective Grading: A Tool for Learning and Assessment...
 HTTP://BOOKS.GOOGLE.COM/BOOKS?ID=EJXY06YX_
 NOC&PRINTSEC=FRONTCOVER&SOURCE=GBS_ATB#V=
 ONEPAGE&Q&F=FALSE

p. 212

90/9/1 rule...
 HTTP://WWW.WIKIPATTERNS.COM/DISPLAY/WIKIPATTERNS/90-
 9-1+THEORY

p. 219

Human-Computer Interaction...
 HTTP://EN.WIKIPEDIA.ORG/WIKI/HUMAN-COMPUTER_
 INTERACTION

Computer-Supported Collaborative Work Systems (CSCW)...
 HTTP://EN.WIKIPEDIA.ORG/WIKI/COMPUTER-SUPPORTED_
 COOPERATIVE_WORK

p. 223

Bloom's Digital Taxonomy Pyramid...
 HTTP://WWW.USI.EDU/DISTANCE/BDT.HTM

p. 224

on Google Docs...
 HTTP://GOO.GL/H02FMA

p. 225

Design principles for tools to support creative thinking...
 HTTP://REPOSITORY.CMU.EDU/ISR/816

Grudin...
 HTTP://WWW.INTERACTION-DESIGN.ORG/REFERENCES/
 AUTHORS/JONATHAN_GRUDIN.HTML

Buxton...
 HTTP://WWW.INTERACTION-DESIGN.ORG/REFERENCES/
 AUTHORS/WILLIAM_BUXTON.HTML

Greenberg...
 HTTP://WWW.INTERACTION-DESIGN.ORG/REFERENCES/
 AUTHORS/SAUL_GREENBERG.HTML

p. 229

Google Docs...
 HTTP://WWW.YOUTUBE.COM/WATCH?V=VVFBQHHKB-K

Google+ Hangouts...
 HTTP://WWW.GOOGLE.COM/+/LEARNMORE/HANGOUTS/

Blackboard Collaborate...
 HTTP://WWW.BLACKBOARD.COM/PLATFORMS/COLLABORATE/
 PRODUCTS/BLACKBOARD-COLLABORATE.ASPX

Adobe Connect...
 HTTP://WWW.ADOBE.COM/PRODUCTS/ADOBECONNECT.HTML

Big Blue Button...

HTTP://WWW.BIGBLUEBUTTON.ORG/
bbs...
HTTP://EN.WIKIPEDIA.ORG/WIKI/BULLETIN_BOARD_SYSTEM

p. 230
guidelines for discussion board writing...
HTTP://WWW.LEHIGH.EDU/~INDISCUS/DOC_GUIDELINES.HTML
shaping a culture of conversation...
HTTP://ACADEMICCOMMONS.ORG/COMMONS/ESSAY/SHAPING-CULTURE-CONVERSATION
This short piece on how to host good conversations online...
HTTP://WWW.RHEINGOLD.COM/TEXTS/ARTONLINEHOST.HTML

p. 231
how forum posts are evaluated...
HTTP://WWW.WPI.EDU/ACADEMICS/ATC/COLLABORATORY/IDEA/BOARDS.HTML

p. 232
David Wooley...
HTTP://THINKOFIT.COM/WHOWEARE.HTM
Forum Software for the Web...
HTTP://THINKOFIT.COM/WEBCONF/FORUMSOFT.HTM
Forum and Message Board Hosting Services...
HTTP://THINKOFIT.COM/WEBCONF/HOSTSITES.HTM
2003 suggestions on how to choose a forum...
HTTPS://DOCS.GOOGLE.COM/DOCUMENT/D/1D606U7SFVD3P7XH0LBF2M001HIDX97R7KVE753HSYEE/EDIT

p. 233
Ward Cunningham...
HTTP://EN.WIKIPEDIA.ORG/WIKI/WARD_CUNNINGHAM
wiki in plain english...
HTTP://WWW.YOUTUBE.COM/WATCH?V=-DNL00TDMLY

p. 234
Google Docs...
HTTPS://DOCS.GOOGLE.COM/
Etherpad...
HTTP://EN.WIKIPEDIA.ORG/WIKI/ETHERPAD
WYSIWYG...
HTTP://EN.WIKIPEDIA.ORG/WIKI/WYSIWYG
wiki markup language...
HTTP://EN.WIKIPEDIA.ORG/WIKI/WIKI_SYNTAX
Hackpad...
HTTPS://HACKPAD.COM/
neutral point of view...
HTTP://EN.WIKIPEDIA.ORG/WIKI/NPOV

p. 235

Mediawiki...
: HTTP://WWW.MEDIAWIKI.ORG/
Tiki...
: HTTP://WWW.TIKI.ORG/
Foswiki...
: HTTP://FOSWIKI.ORG/

p. 236
wiki farm...
: HTTP://EN.WIKIPEDIA.ORG/WIKI/WIKI_HOSTING_SERVICE
Wikimatrix...
: HTTP://WWW.WIKIMATRIX.ORG/
Here...
: HTTP://C2.COM/CGI/WIKI?TOPTENWIKIENGINES

p. 237
Massive Open Online Courses (MOOCs)...
: HTTP://SOCIALMEDIACLASSROOM.COM/HOST/PEERAGOGY/WIKI/CONNECTIVISM-PRACTICE-HOW-ORGANIZE-A-MOOC
learning context...
: HTTP://SOCIALMEDIACLASSROOM.COM/HOST/PEERAGOGY/WIKI/ORGANIZING-A-LEARNING-CONTEXT
Wikipedia...
: HTTP://WWW.WIKIPEDIA.ORG/
connectivism...
: HTTP://EN.WIKIPEDIA.ORG/WIKI/CONNECTIVISM
Diigo link...
: HTTP://WWW.DIIGO.COM/USER/REGISB/WIKI%20EDUCATION

p. 238
Appropedia...
: HTTP://WWW.APPROPEDIA.ORG/WELCOME_TO_APPROPEDIA
sustainability...
: HTTP://WWW.APPROPEDIA.ORG/SUSTAINABILITY
poverty...
: HTTP://WWW.APPROPEDIA.ORG/POVERTY
international development...
: HTTP://WWW.APPROPEDIA.ORG/INTERNATIONAL_DEVELOPMENT
principles...
: HTTP://WWW.APPROPEDIA.ORG/PRINCIPLES
appropriate technology...
: HTTP://WWW.APPROPEDIA.ORG/APPROPRIATE_TECHNOLOGY
project...
: HTTP://WWW.APPROPEDIA.ORG/PROJECT
Teahouse...
: HTTP://EN.WIKIPEDIA.ORG/WIKI/WIKIPEDIA:TEAHOUSE

p. 239

Wiki...
  HTTP://EN.WIKIPEDIA.ORG/WIKI/WIKI
Toward a complex adaptative intelligence community - The wiki and the blog...
  HTTP://SSRN.COM/ABSTRACT=755904
La gestion de projet croise le wiki...
  HTTP://WWW.REGISBARONDEAU.COM/CHAPITRE+4%3A+ANALYSE+DU+CAS#SYNTH_SE

p. 242
Blackboard Collaborate...
  HTTP://WWW.BLACKBOARD.COM/PLATFORMS/COLLABORATE/OVERVIEW.ASPX
Adobe Connect...
  HTTP://WWW.ADOBE.COM/PRODUCTS/ADOBECONNECT/FEATURES.HTML
Google+ Hangout...
  HTTP://WWW.GOOGLE.COM/+/LEARNMORE/HANGOUTS/
Skype...
  HTTP://WWW.SKYPE.COM
Mumble...
  HTTP://MUMBLE.SOURCEFORGE.NET/
Big Blue Button...
  HTTP://WWW.BIGBLUEBUTTON.ORG/
Big Marker...
  HTTP://WWW.BIGMARKER.COM/ABOUT
Dim-Dim...
  HTTP://WWW.DIMDIM.COM
Howard Rheingold's...
  HTTP://DELICIOUS.COM/HRHEINGOLD/WEBCONFERENCING
Robin Good'...
  HTTP://WWW.MINDMEISTER.COM/12213323/BEST-ONLINE-COLLABORATION-TOOLS-2012-ROBIN-GOOD-S-COLLABORATIVE-MAP

p. 243
Etherpad...
  HTTP://ETHERPAD.ORG

p. 244
Google+ Hangout...
  HTTP://LIFEHACKER.COM/5842191/GOOGLE%252B-HANGOUTS-ADDS-SCREEN-SHARING-GOOGLE-DOCS-COLLABORATION-AND-MORE
stream a Hangout and record it to YouTube...
  HTTP://WWW.GOOGLE.COM/+/LEARNMORE/HANGOUTS/ONAIR.HTML

p. 246
> Teaching smart people how to learn...
>> HTTP://PDS8.EGLOOS.COM/PDS/200805/20/87/CHRIS_ARGYRIS_LEARNING.PDF

p. 249
> Howard Rheingold...
>> HTTP://EN.WIKIPEDIA.ORG/WIKI/HOWARD_RHEINGOLD
>
> Amanda Lyons...
>> HTTP://WWW.VISUALSFORCHANGE.COM/
>
> Howard Rheingold's...
>> HTTP://RHEINGOLD.COM/
>
> Regents Lecture...
>> HTTP://VIMEO.COM/35685124
>
> our website...
>> PEERAGOGY.ORG
>
> print on demand...
>> HTTP://WWW.LULU.COM/SHOP/HOWARD-RHEINGOLD-AND-PEERAGOGYORG-EDITORS/THE-PEERAGOGY-HANDBOOK/PAPERBACK/PRODUCT-20607425.HTML
>
> free PDF...
>> HTTP://METAMESO.ORG/PEERAGOGY-2.0-EBOOK.PDF
>
> Google+ community...
>> HTTPS://PLUS.GOOGLE.COM/U/0/COMMUNITIES/107386162349686249470

p. 250
> YouTube Channel...
>> HTTP://WWW.YOUTUBE.COM/CHANNEL/UCIQY4JA8E4BR-I9U5KNMYZQ
>
> grow concept maps,...
>> HTTP://CMAPSPUBLIC3.IHMC.US/RID=1K81VLSK7-1RL0RQ4-WZK/PEERAGOGY%20CMAP.CMAP
>
> this Diigo group...
>> HTTP://GROUPS.DIIGO.COM/GROUP/PEERAGOGY-HANDBOOK
>
> this one...
>> HTTP://GROUPS.DIIGO.COM/GROUP/PEERING-INTO-PEERAGOGY%20

p. 251
> this Google Doc...
>> HTTPS://DOCS.GOOGLE.COM/DOCUMENT/D/1_2I-Z-PT5NUKK-FPY4JSQXFEXBWS4AO4SIHKXCCRVEI/EDIT#

p. 255
> Implementing Paragogy...
>> HTTPS://EN.WIKIVERSITY.ORG/WIKI/USER:ARIDED/IMPLEMENTINGPARAGOGY

Wikipedia page...
> HTTP://EN.WIKIPEDIA.ORG/WIKI/PEER_LEARNING

p. 258
Why software should be free...
> HTTP://WWW.GNU.ORG/PHILOSOPHY/SHOULDBEFREE.HTML

p. 261
The Contribution of Judo to Education...
> HTTP://JUDOINFO.COM/KANO.HTM

p. 262
The Timeless Way of Building...
> HTTP://EN.WIKIPEDIA.ORG/WIKI/THE_TIMELESS_WAY_OF_BUILDING

here...
> HTTPS://PLUS.GOOGLE.COM/U/0/108598104736826154120/POSTS/AGWYCQPHQSN

Wikipatterns...
> HTTP://WWW.WIKIPATTERNS.COM/DISPLAY/WIKIPATTERNS/ABOUT

The Origins of Pattern Theory, the Future of the Theory, And The Generation of a Living World...
> HTTP://WWW.PATTERNLANGUAGE.COM/ARCHIVE/IEEE/IEEETEXT.HTM

Cluetrain Manifesto...
> HTTP://WWW.CLUETRAIN.COM

First edition...
> HTTP://WWW.CLUETRAIN.COM/BOOK/INDEX.HTML

New Rules for the New Economy...
> HTTP://WWW.KK.ORG/NEWRULES/CONTENTS.PHP

(you can also...
> HTTP://WWW.KK.ORG/NEWRULES/CONTENTS.PHP

read the book online...
> HTTP://WWW.KK.ORG/NEWRULES/CONTENTS.PHP

p. 263
Why do newcomers abandon open source software projects?...
> HTTP://LAPESSC.IME.USP.BR/PUBLIC/PAPERS/13872/CHASE13_PRESENT.PDF

Sapir-Whorf Hypothesis...
> HTTP://EN.WIKIPEDIA.ORG/WIKI/LINGUISTIC_RELATIVITY

symbolic violence...
> HTTP://EN.WIKIPEDIA.ORG/WIKI/SYMBOLIC_VIOLENCE

These fifteen properties are the glue which binds wholeness together...
> HTTP://WWW.LIVINGNEIGHBORHOODS.ORG/HT-0/FIFTEEN.HTM

manga fan groups co-learning Japanese...
> HTTP://MITPRESS.MIT.EDU/BOOKS/FULL_PDFS/HANGING_OUT.

PDF
MindAmp groups...
   http://socialmediaclassroom.com/host/mindamp5/lockedwiki/main-page
Creativity support tools: accelerating discovery and innovation...
   http://doi.acm.org/10.1145/1323688.1323689
Summary...
   http://david.lasindias.com/phyles/
Book...
   http://deugarte.com/gomi/phyles.pdf

p. 264
Video...
   http://www.google.com/search?client=chrome-mobile&sourceid=chrome-mobile&ie=UTF-8&q=Of+Conflict+in+Virtual+Learning+Communiities+in+the+Context+of+a+Democratic+Pedagogy
text...
   http://networkedlearningconference.org.uk/abstracts/pdf/ozturk.pdf
How a Class Becomes a Community...
   http://news.rapgenius.com/Cathy-davidson-how-a-class-becomes-a-community-theory-method-examples-chapter-one-lyrics
Richard Byrne...
   http://www.freetech4teachers.com/
Sylvia Tolisano...
   http://langwitches.org/blog/
Caitlin Tucker...
   http://catlintucker.com/2011/11/12-tech-tools-that-will-transform-your-classroom/
Vicki Davis...
   http://coolcatteacher.blogspot.ca/
Degrees of Connected Teaching...
   %20http://thecleversheep.blogspot.ca/2012/06/seven-degrees-of-connectedness_06.html
TeachThought...
   %20http://thecleversheep.blogspot.ca/2012/06/seven-degrees-of-connectedness_06.html
David Truss...
   http://pairadimes.davidtruss.com/

p. 265
Steven Downes...
   http://www.downes.ca/presentation/264
Will Richardson...

HTTP://WILLRICHARDSON.COM/
The d.school Bootcamp Bootleg...
    HTTP://DSCHOOL.STANFORD.EDU/WP-CONTENT/UPLOADS/2011/
    03/BOOTCAMPBOOTLEG2010V2SLIM.PDF
MOOC site...
    HTTP://CHANGE.MOOC.CA
What Connectivism Is...
    HTTP://HALFANHOUR.BLOGSPOT.COM/2007/02/WHAT-
    CONNECTIVISM-IS.HTML
An Introduction to Connective Knowledge...
    HTTP://WWW.DOWNES.CA/POST/33034
Facilitating a Massive Open Online Course...
    HTTP://WWW.DOWNES.CA/PRESENTATION/290
gRSShopper...
    HTTP://GRSSHOPPER.DOWNES.CA/INDEX.HTML
Connectivism: A Learning Theory for the Digital Age...
    %20HTTP://WWW.ELEARNSPACE.ORG/ARTICLES/CONNECTIVISM.
    HTM
A Connectivism Glossary...
    HTTP://EN.WIKIVERSITY.ORG/WIKI/CONNECTIVISM_GLOSSARY
Rhizomes and Networks...
    HTTP://WWW.CONNECTIVISM.CA/?P=329
Rhizomatic Education: Community as Curriculum...
    HTTP://INNOVATEONLINE.INFO/PDF/VOL4_ISSUE5/
    RHIZOMATIC_EDUCATION-__COMMUNITY_AS_CURRICULUM.PDF
Knowing Knowledge...
    HTTP://WWW.AMAZON.CA/KNOWING-KNOWLEDGE-GEORGE-
    SIEMENS/DP/1430302305

p. 266

Net Smart,...
    HTTP://WWW.AMAZON.COM/NET-SMART-EBOOK/DP/B007D5UP9G
Massive Open Online Courses...
    HTTP://WWW.LEARNINGSOLUTIONSMAG.COM/ARTICLES/886/
The MOOC guide...
    HTTPS://SITES.GOOGLE.COM/SITE/THEMOOCGUIDE/
Peer Education: Training of Trainers Manual...
    HTTP://WWW.SCRIBD.COM/DOC/54544925/51/TRAINING-TOPIC-
    CO-FACILITATION-SKILLS
Co Facilitating...
    HTTP://WWW.BREAKOUTOFTHEBOX.COM/CO-
    FACILITATINGPFEIFFERJONES.PDF
Summary...
    HTTP://REVIEWING.CO.UK/ARCHIVES/ART/13_1_WHAT_DO_
    FACILITATORS_DO.HTM#8_WAYS_OF_FACILITATING_ACTIVE_

LEARNING
Carl Rogers, Core Conditions and Education...
    HTTP://WWW.INFED.ORG/THINKERS/ET-ROGERS.HTM
Peer Mediation...
    HTTP://WWW.STUDYGS.NET/PEERMED.HTM
Co-Facilitation: The Advantages and Challenges...
    HTTP://SK.CUPE.CA/UPDIR/COFACILITATION-HANDOUTS.DOC
Bohemia Interactive Community Wiki Guidelines...
    HTTP://COMMUNITY.BISTUDIO.COM/WIKI/BOHEMIA_
    INTERACTIVE_COMMUNITY:GUIDELINES
Carl Roger's Helping System. Journey and Substance...
    HTTP://OPENLIBRARY.ORG/WORKS/OL2014352W/CARL_ROGERS'
    _HELPING_SYSTEM
5 Pillars of Wikipedia...
    HTTP://EN.WIKIPEDIA.ORG/W/INDEX.PHP?TITLE=WIKIPEDIA:
    FIVE_PILLARS&OLDID=501472166
Training the Force...
    HTTP://WWW.AFRICOM.MIL/WO-NCO/DOWNLOADCENTER/
    %5C40PUBLICATIONS/TRAINING%20THE%20FORCE%20MANUAL.PDF
Learning Reimagined: Participatory, Peer, Global, Online...
    HTTP://DMLCENTRAL.NET/BLOG/HOWARD-RHEINGOLD/
    LEARNING-REIMAGINED-PARTICIPATORY-PEER-GLOBAL-ONLINE
Research Gate...
    HTTP://WWW.RESEARCHGATE.NET/

p. 267
Creating and Facilitating Peer Support Groups...
    HTTP://CTB.KU.EDU/EN/TABLECONTENTS/SECTION_1180.ASPX
Facilitation Tips...
    HTTP://WWW1.VILLANOVA.EDU/CONTENT/VILLANOVA/ARTSCI/
    VCLE/RESOURCES/TOOLKIT/_JCR_CONTENT/PAGECONTENT/
    DOWNLOAD_8/FILE.RES/FACILITATIONTIPS.DOC
Herding Passionate Cats: The Role of Facilitator in a Peer Learning...
    HTTP://PIPPABUCHANAN.COM/2011/09/04/HERDING-
    PASSIONATE-CATS-THE-ROLE-OF-FACILITATOR-IN-A-PEER-
    LEARNING-PROCESS/
Reflective Peer Facilitation: Crafting Collaborative Self-Assessment...
    HTTP://WEBPAGES.SOU.EDU/~VIDMAR/SOARS2008/VIDMAR.PPT
Effective Co-Facilitation...
    HTTP://WWW.UMASS.EDU/EWC/EA/FACILITATION%20SKILLS/
    IMPORTANT%20TIPS.DOC
Teaching smart people how to learn...
    WWW.NCSU.EDU/PARK_SCHOLARSHIPS/PDF/CHRIS_ARGYRIS_
    LEARNING.PDF?
book...

HTTP://WWW.AMAZON.COM/TEACHING-PEOPLE-HARVARD-BUSINESS-CLASSICS/DP/1422126005

Assessing Open and distance learners....
HTTP://WWW.AMAZON.COM/ASSESSING-DISTANCE-LEARNERS-FLEXIBLE-LEARNING/DP/0749428783/REF=TMM_PAP_TITLE_0?IE=UTF8&QID=1388199564&SR=1-1

Peer-To-Peer Recognition of Learning in Open Education...
HTTP://WWW.IRRODL.ORG/INDEX.PHP/IRRODL/ARTICLE/VIEW/641/1389

Mind in Society: Development of Higher Psychological Processes...
HTTP://BOOKS.GOOGLE.COM/BOOKS?ID=RXJJUEFZE_OC&PRINTSEC=FRONTCOVER&SOURCE=GBS_ATB#V=ONEPAGE&Q&F=FALSE

Reijo Miettinen...
HTTP://ORG.SAGEPUB.COM/SEARCH?AUTHOR1=REIJO+MIETTINEN&SORTSPEC=DATE&SUBMIT=SUBMIT

Jaakko Virkkunen...
HTTP://ORG.SAGEPUB.COM/SEARCH?AUTHOR1=JAAKKO+VIRKKUNEN&SORTSPEC=DATE&SUBMIT=SUBMIT

Epistemic Objects, Artifacts and Organizational Change...
HTTP://ORG.SAGEPUB.COM/CONTENT/12/3/437.ABSTRACT

p. 268

bookmarks...
HTTP://DELICIOUS.COM/HRHEINGOLD/WEBCONFERENCING

p. 269

Why use forums?...
HTTP://BLIP.TV/FILE/1123048

The Art of Hosting Good Conversations Online...
HTTP://WWW.RHEINGOLD.COM/TEXTS/ARTONLINEHOST.HTML

Guidelines for Discussion Board Writing...
HTTP://WWW.LEHIGH.EDU/~INDISCUS/DOC_GUIDELINES.HTML

Shaping a culture of conversation. The discussion board and beyond...
HTTP://WWW.ACADEMICCOMMONS.ORG/2009/01/SHAPING-A-CULTURE-OF-CONVERSATION-THE-DISCUSSION-BOARD-AND-BEYOND/

Improving the Use of Discussion Boards...
HTTP://WWW.WPI.EDU/ACADEMICS/ATC/COLLABORATORY/IDEA/BOARDS.HTML

Implementing Paragogy...
HTTP://METAMESO.ORG/~JOE/DOCS/PARAGOGY-LESSON.PDF

Is it time for a BYOL (Bring Your Own Learning) strategy for your organization?...
HTTP://WWW.C4LPT.CO.UK/BLOG/2012/04/20/IS-IT-TIME-FOR-A-BYOL-BRING-YOUR-OWN-LEARNING-STRATEGY-IN-

YOUR-ORGANIZATION-BYOL/

Shelly Terrell: Global Netweaver, Curator, PLN Builder....
HTTP://DMLCENTRAL.NET/BLOG/HOWARD-RHEINGOLD/SHELLY-TERRELL-GLOBAL-NETWEAVER-CURATOR-PLN-BUILDER

Personal Learning Networks: Using the Power of Connection to Transform Education...
HTTP://WWW.AMAZON.COM/PERSONAL-LEARNING-NETWORKS-CONNECTIONS-TRANSFORM/DP/193554327X

p. 270

Constructivism...
HTTP://EN.WIKIPEDIA.ORG/WIKI/CONSTRUCTIVISM_(PHILOSOPHY_OF_EDUCATION)

Social constructivism...
HTTP://EN.WIKIPEDIA.ORG/WIKI/SOCIAL_CONSTRUCTIVISM

Radical constructivism...
HTTP://WWW.ENGLISH.IUP.EDU/MMWIMSON/SYLLABI/803/721/RADICAL%20CONSTRUCTIVISM%20%20%20721.HTM

Enactivism...
HTTP://EN.WIKIPEDIA.ORG/WIKI/ENACTIVISM_(PSYCHOLOGY)

Constructionism...
HTTP://EN.WIKIPEDIA.ORG/WIKI/CONSTRUCTIONISM_(LEARNING_THEORY)

Connectivism...
HTTP://EN.WIKIPEDIA.ORG/WIKI/CONNECTIVISM

p. 271

self-organizing...
HTTP://EN.WIKIPEDIA.ORG/WIKI/SELF-ORGANIZATION

p. 275

Bronx Academy Senior High...
HTTP://BRONXBASH.COM

New York City Writing Project...
HTTP://NYCWRITINGPROJECT.ORG

National Writing Project...
HTTP://NWP.ORG

Youth Voices...
HTTP://YOUTHVOICES.NET%20

Teachers Teaching Teachers...
HTTP://TEACHERSTEACHINGTEACHERS.ORG

p. 278

Internet Time Alliance...
HTTP://INTERNETTIMEALLIANCE.COM/

p. 309

Creative Commons 0 copyright waiver...
HTTP://CREATIVECOMMONS.ORG/PUBLICDOMAIN/ZERO/1.0/

CHAPTER 38

LICENSE/WAIVER

These materials are made available under the terms of CREATIVE COMMONS 0 COPYRIGHT WAIVER instead of a "traditional" copyleft license. We the undersigned agree to the following, wherein "this work" refers to "The Peeragogy Handbook" and all other content posted on peeragogy.org or the original collaboratory site, socialmediaclassroom.com/host/peeragogy.

I hereby waive all copyright and related or neighboring rights together with all associated claims and causes of action with respect to this work to the extent possible under the law.

Signed:

- Bryan Alexander
- Paul Allison
- Régis Barondeau
- Doug Breitbart
- George Brett
- Suz Burroughs
- Teryl Cartwright
- Joseph Corneli
- Jay Cross
- Charles Jeffrey Danoff
- Julian Elve

- María Fernanda
- James Folkestad
- John Glass
- Kathy Gill
- John Graves
- Gigi Johnson
- Anna Keune
- Kyle Larson
- Roland Legrand
- Amanda Lyons
- Christopher Tillman Neal
- Ted Newcomb
- Stephanie Parker
- Charlotte Pierce
- David Preston
- Howard Rheingold
- Paola Ricaurte
- Verena Roberts
- Stephanie Schipper
- Peter Taylor
- Fabrizio Terzi
- Geoff Walker

Note that this waiver does not apply to other works by the above authors, including works linked to from peeragogy.org. It also does not apply to embedded content drawn from other sites and included for the reader's convenience.

Future contributors: Note also that we will require a similar copyright waiver agreement from you. That said, the waiver also means that you are free to do essentially whatever you like with the content in your own work! Have fun!

How we came to this decision

These Creative Commons license options were proposed by various members of the community:

- *CC Zero* - public domain; no restrictions for downstream users

- *CC By-SA* - requires downstream users to include attribution and to license their work in the same way

- *CC By-SA-NC* - requires downstream users to include attribution, to license their work in the same way and disallows any commercial use of the content

After a brief discussion, no one was in favor of restricting downstream users, so we decided to go with CC0. We agreed that we would get enough "credit" by having our names on peeragogy.org. In connection with this discussion, we agreed that we would work on ways to explicitly build "reusability" into the handbook content.